ARE YOU READY FOR LOVE?

The following questionnaire is just one of the many personalized quizzes included in this remarkable book. Check off the statements which apply to *you*—and discover what you're *really* looking for in the game of love . . .

_____ I first need to know myself before I reach out for a meaningful relationship.

_____ I'm not perfect so why do I keep looking for the perfect relationship?

_____ It is important that I treat my lover as my best friend.

_____ The right man/woman will appear when the time is right.

_____ I'll _____ sitting around

_____ _____ eone to take

_____ ___ng love doesn't come automatically. It takes time and a concrete plan.

Are you ready for love? Analyze your own responses in this practical guide—and let Sally Jessy Raphael show you the easy way to finding romance in today's world . . .

FINDING LOVE

FINDING LOVE

PRACTICAL ADVICE
FOR
MEN AND WOMEN

AMERICA'S #1 T.V. AND RADIO ADVICE COLUMNIST

SALLY JESSY RAPHAEL

AND
M. J. ABADIE

JOVE BOOKS, NEW YORK

This Jove book contains the revised
text of the original edition.
It has been completely reset in a typeface
designed for easy reading and was printed
from new film.

FINDING LOVE

A Jove Book / published by arrangement with
the authors

PRINTING HISTORY
Arbor House edition / August 1984
Published in Canada by Fitzhenry & Whiteside, Ltd.
Jove edition / June 1988

ISBN: 0-515-09796-9

Jove Books are published by The Berkley Publishing Group,
200 Madison Avenue, New York, New York 10016.
The name ''JOVE'' and the ''J'' logo
are trademarks belonging to Jove Publications, Inc.

PRINTED IN THE UNITED STATES OF AMERICA

10 9 8 7 6 5 4 3 2 1

Acknowledgments

As I'm not a professional writer, this may be the only chance I'll ever get to say "thank you" in print to those who have been important along the way.

I am a dream of my mother, Dede, and she is always with me, as are my father, Jesse, and my brother, Steve. They were my foundation.

Allison and Andrea, my daughters, shared the journey as did J.J., my son. Although our road was sometimes rough, we never despaired because we knew we had each other to the end. Other members of my family—Barrie, Midge, Nancy, Steve, Allen, and Lynne—deserve recognition for their steady presence.

And I want to thank my friends Jay, Sandy, Rose, Linda, Harriet, Sharon, and Arlene for their continuing encouragement.

To those who believed in my work, an especial appreciation: to the gentlemen—and they are gentlemen!—of Multi-Media: Walter Bartlett; Dick Thrall; Jim Lynagh; Peter Lund; and Burt Dubrow, the only knight I ever met; to Maurice Tunick of ABC radio network; and to Biggie Navins, in memory. We are a team. To them, a heartfelt thanks.

To the men I have loved and who have loved me, a gracious bow for their warmth and support: Ron, Neil, Art, and Harold.

And to Karl Soderlund I'd like to say, "As long as you're there, all men will have something to live up to."

I want to thank Fate for sending me a true professional

vi Acknowledgments

writer as my coauthor, M. J. Abadie. I didn't believe it possible to have a collaboration in such perfect understanding and accord—all through the difficult work there was not a cloud.

She and I both wish to acknowledge those who generously shared their experiences: Diane Pra Sisto, Francine Kern, John Gottfried, and Rick Croll; and others without whose faith and support this book might not have seen the light: Lilly Hirshon, Timothy Menton, and Gregory Mowery—all essential links in the chain of loving help. Mark Hasselriis provided a valuable and insightful critique.

Our sincere appreciation goes to our editor Sallye Leventhal, for her warmth and imagination in handling the editorial tasks of this edition.

Our agents, Sherry Robb and Bart Andrews, come in for a big hurrah. Not only did they have the perspicacity to imagine this book, they had the foresight to create the collaboration that brought it forth.

The list would not be complete without my thanking all of my listeners and viewers who, in sharing their joys and tribulations, were my true inspiration.

S.J.R.
M.J.A.

CONTENTS

INTRODUCTION

Hi! I'm Sally Jessy Raphael.

Every weekday night over ABC network radio this is how I introduce myself to my listeners who call to ask my advice. What I've learned by answering America's questions five nights a week is that almost everybody is searching for love.

For centuries, marriages were made chiefly for social, financial, or political reasons, rarely for romance (or for sex, for that matter). Matters of the heart were relegated to the status of frivolity. Romantic love took a back seat to preserving the family unit and producing children and was largely assumed to be expendable and even detrimental to the marriage union and the social order. Indeed, love was not considered a fit topic for the attention of anyone past adolescence. People were told to put away "childish dreams" when they married, to get on with the serious business of life—making money and raising children.

Until quite recently, love was a very different proposition for the two sexes. For women, it was a rather sweet and passive thing, equated with the love of home and children. Men were presumed to be "interested in only one thing,'' and were not only permitted to indulge in sex outside of marriage but actively *encouraged* to do so in order to spare the feelings of their ''proper'' and ''delicate'' wives. Women were either ''good'' or ''bad.'' The good ones did not enjoy sex, but tolerated it for the sake of childbearing. And men simply didn't *marry* the bad women.

All of that has changed. In the wake of women's liberation we have learned not only that ''nice girls do,'' but that they want more. Women are starved for romantic love. Numerous psychological and social studies have shown that men, too, yearn for feelings of tenderness and rapport in their relationships. As the traditional ''macho'' male image fades, men are eagerly investigating the *feeling* side of sex.

In addition, both sexes are learning that we are all unique individuals, not ''roles'' we play. With safe and reliable birth control available to all, sex-for-procreation is your choice. These factors have combined to release powerful new expectations of love—and a widespread desire to experience the fusion of emotional and sexual fulfillment.

No longer are the majority content to settle for a loveless, if safe, relationship just to assure the basic necessities of life or to avoid confronting it alone. The married, too, are reaching out to bring love into their lives before it is too late. Divorce is still on the increase. As more and more women become at least partially self-supporting, their demand for love increases. And as men come to understand that a woman who is more than a sexually available housekeeper can enrich their lives immeasurably, they, too, are demanding the emotional rewards traditionally reserved for women.

Whereas once the course of life was laid out precisely (and one had only to follow its prescribed way to be, if not happy, at least socially secure and acceptable), now people imagine that satisfying sex and love *can* be realized in one relationship. This idea has become a major focus for many people's lives. I view this as a step in the right direction, but now freedoms bring problems. No longer clear on what constitutes a "good" relationship, people are groping for love without proper information, or with misinformation. Many are finding themselves in a relationship formed for the wrong reasons.

The turbulent 1970s were propelled by the quest for sexual freedom, and we are now suffering the consequences of those times. The one-night stand, so much a part of those years, is now giving way to a desire for more intimate, solid relationships, as casual sex, once a badge of freedom, has taken on ominous overtones with the advent of sexually transmitted diseases, especially AIDS. More than ever, people are looking for *love,* especially as a prerequisite of sex. Today we need to know more about *ourselves* and *others* before embarking on the romantic quest.

The Number One question I'm asked on the air is, "Sally, how do I find love?" No question about it, the one-on-one committed relationship is *the* issue of the day. And America's quest for love has just begun.

I have discovered that most people don't know *what* love is, *when* to look for it, *why* they want it, or *how* to find it. Therefore, I am going to provide you with some information . . . and try to answer for each of you the question, "How do I find love?" People *rely* on my advice—not because it's profound, but because it's *practical.* I've been married and divorced, I've loved well and badly, I've raised children, I'm a business woman, and, perhaps most important, I'm now in a happy, committed relationship.

I don't pull any punches. Before I was a TV and radio host I was an investigative reporter, so I'm used to dealing in specifics. The information you'll find in this book is based on facts and lots of research. I hope it's not some pie-in-the-sky theoretical nonsense. I've seen these ideas *work:* I've tried them myself.

Starting off with some questionnaires, I'm going to ask

you to rate yourself . . . to get On Your Mark. Then, I'm going to tell you how to Get Set, Get Ready, and Go!

After you've determined from answering my little quiz *(honestly!)* that you really want to find love, I'm going to show you how to find exactly what you're looking for. Expect some surprises. Many of us only *think* we know what we are looking for—that's what causes a lot of trouble and disappointment.

After the "why-you-are-looking-for-love" and "what-you-are-looking-for" are settled, we'll go on to examine where and when to look.

Then comes the all-important "how." I'll be letting you in on some special techniques, including my own "Sally's Basic Rules," and showing you how to capitalize on your unique self.

I'm going to tell you how to go it alone and find love. We'll talk about how to cope with the danger of rejection (always there) as well as the other side of the coin—how to get rid of somebody you don't want. And I'll show you how to design your own personal game plan for finding love.

Love is always walking by, but if you're not ready to grab it, it'll just keep on walkin'. If you want someone *wonderful,* then you've got to put time and work into being *wonderful* yourself.

That's what my book is all about.

PART ONE

PRELIMINARIES

1

On Your Mark

Are you ready for love?

It's a deceptively simple question. You might think right off that the answer is *yes*. Why else would you be reading this book, right? It's not that easy.

In fact, I'd be willing to bet that fifty percent of you *aren't* ready. *What!* you may say, or, *Sally, that's crazy,* everybody's *looking for love. True,* I'd answer. *Everybody's* looking *for love, but—and this is a big BUT—everybody isn't ready to find love!*

How do you know if you are ready for love? We're going to cover quite a few points to determine that. And if after taking the following questionnaire and scoring yourself (remember—be honest) you can truthfully say you're *ready,* then go right on reading. You're going to have to make a serious commitment to this project, and you're going to have to follow my plan step-by-step. No skipping. No excuses. I'm going to bet that it will work for you. But only if *you* will work for *you.*

If you find out after taking the questionnaire that you're not as ready as you thought you were, read on. You'll learn how to get ready—exactly what steps to take, and in what order. Remember, this is a *practical* guide. We're in this together. I want you to succeed.

Is finding love my first priority? You may respond with an immediate yes without really thinking realistically about the time and energy involved in finding the perfect mate.

Below is a five-part series of mini-questionnaires. Check all the questions and comments that relate to you. If some don't reflect your attitudes or feelings, simply leave them blank, but be sure your answers reflect your *true* attitude, not what you think you're *supposed* to feel. If a question applies only partially, check the answer that comes closest.

Use the evaluation form below each mini-questionnaire to figure out your own score. At the end of all five questionnaires you will add up your total score and that will tell you whether you are truly On Your Mark.

Instructions: For every question/comment you checked on the left, mark the following values in the right column. (Give one point for an A, two points for a B, and for a C give yourself three points.) Add up your right column and put down your total for Mini-Questionnaire #1.

MINI-QUESTIONNAIRE #1

General Attitude

_____ I first need to know myself before I reach _____
out for a meaningful relationship.(A)

_____ I'm not perfect so why do I keep looking _____
for the perfect relationship? (B)

_____ I'm bored being alone.(B) _____

_____ If we're not the same religion the rela- _____
tionship doesn't seem to last.(B)

_____ I am looking for a mate who will rescue
me from my own personal problems.(C)

_____ I am no good alone. I need someone to _____
take care of me.(C)

_____ It is important that I treat my lover as _____
my best friend.(A)

_____ Financial security is everything to me and _____
is the first thing I look for in a partner
even if I don't feel like I'm in love.(C)

_____ Finding love doesn't come automatically. _____
It takes time and a concrete plan.(A)

_____ Love can begin with a chance meeting _____
but won't develop without nurture.(B)

_____ I do not want a lifetime mate.(C) _____

_____ I'll never find a relationship sitting around _____
and dreaming about it.(A)

_____ The right man/woman will appear when _____
the time is right.(C)

_____ A solid and lasting relationship takes time _____
to develop.(A)

MINI-QUESTIONNAIRE #2

Work World vs. Personal Life

_____ I am so exhausted by the end of the day that all I want to do is curl up with a good book and go to bed early. (C) _____

_____ Right now work is my priority.(C) _____

_____ My work is very isolating and I get "people starved," so I try to go out and socialize as much as possible.(B) _____

_____ Between my job and my friends I have all the loving relationships I need.(C) _____

_____ I spend as much time working on finding a relationship as I do on my work activities.(A) _____

_____ I deal with so many people each day that my idea of a perfect evening is sitting home alone with a drink in one hand and my TV remote in the other. (C) _____

_____ I would be willing to change jobs or even relocate if the right relationship came along.(A) _____

_____ I work so hard just trying to survive that "working" on a relationship is more than I could bear right now.(C) _____

_____ The perfect ending to the day would be _____
to come home to that very special someone.(A)

_____ My main goal in life is to find a lasting _____
relationship.(A)

MINI-QUESTIONNAIRE #3

Past Relationships

_____ True love is too painful, so I will settle for a relationship of convenience.(C) _____

_____ I have found that I am not a full person without that special someone in my life. (B) _____

_____ I am willing to take a serious look at what went wrong in my last relationship and how I could have made it better. (A) _____

_____ I am not willing to set myself up for another rejection.(C) _____

_____ My husband/wife and I split up. I don't know where or how to begin to find a new relationship.(B) _____

_____ All the men/women I go out with want sex, but none of them seem to want a permanent relationship.(C) _____

_____ I spent most of my time raising the children alone and now that they are all gone my life feels empty. I've almost forgotten how to socialize with adults. (B) _____

_____ My own identity is a little shaken so I want to get my own act together before looking for a relationship.(B) _____

_____ After dating so many men/women I know exactly what I am *not* looking for.(B) _____

_____ I am alone because no one cares.(C) _____

_____ My husband/wife recently died and I'm trying to get my life back into order.(B) _____

_____ The only way that I feel like a whole person is in contact with another.(C) _____

_____ My last relationship ended so miserably that I'm afraid to try another one so soon.(C) _____

_____ I am alone because I just never found the right man/woman.(B) _____

_____ I've never really sat down and made a list of the qualities I am looking for in a mate.(C) _____

_____ I've been alone and happy with myself. I only want a relationship if it can add new and loving dimensions to my life.(A) _____

_____ I am a very busy person. Another person would have to fit into my schedule. (B) _____

MINI-QUESTIONNAIRE #4

Family/Friends Pressure

_____ My relatives keep asking me, "When are you going to get married?" They won't get off my back until I do.(C) _____

_____ All my friends are getting married and I feel left out.(C) _____

_____ I am desperate for a relationship before it gets too late.(C) _____

_____ It's never too late to find a relationship and I'm never too old to stop looking. (A) _____

_____ My idea of a perfect mate is someone just like dad/mom.(C) _____

_____ No one wants to fall in love with a woman/man with a family. I won't find a partner willing to take me and my children as his/her responsibility.(C) _____

_____ My friends think that I am nobody since I don't have a serious relationship.(C) _____

_____ I'm in my thirties and really want to have a child before it is too late. I'm also willing to wait for the right, loving mate. (A) _____

_____ My mother thinks it's time for me to get married.(C) _____

_____ It doesn't matter what my family or my   _____
      friends think. It's my life and my rela-
      tionship and I'll take my time.(A)

_____ It's okay to be alone but it would be   _____
      better if I could find that other person
      who wanted love as much as I do.(A)

_____ I need to spend a lot of time with my   _____
      family/friends.(C)

_____ I couldn't possibly fall in love with some- _____
      one of a different background (religion
      or race).(C)

_____ I'd consider anyone of any background   _____
      who met my general values.(A)

_____ Education means a lot to me. Someone   _____
      of a lesser status would make me uncom-
      fortable.(B)

_____ I don't mind what a person does for a   _____
      living so long as he/she is nice and de-
      cent and we have things in common.(A)

MINI-QUESTIONNAIRE #5

Health/Finances/Activities

_____ I am not physically fit and I don't feel good about myself.(C)   _____

_____ I take care of myself and am sure I get the proper nutrition, exercise and sleep.(A)   _____

_____ Even if I have to skip a few meals I am sure to save money for a regular haircut and enough for weekly entertainment.(A)   _____

_____ I don't go anywhere unless I look my best.(A)   _____

_____ I always intend on getting dressed up and going out over the weekend, but usually end up sitting at home in my jeans or sweats.(C)   _____

_____ I always try to wear clothes that emphasize my best physical features and ones that reflect my personality. (A)   _____

_____ I'm not very adventurous and am afraid to take chances. Meeting new people is not comfortable so I don't go out.(C)   _____

_____ I meet a few people, give them my number and then stay home waiting for the phone to ring.(B)   _____

_____ Each week one of my favorite pastimes is to figure out creative new places and new ways to meet men/women.(A)   _____

_____   I'm so sick of bars, and those are the   _____
only places you can meet men/women.
(C)

_____   I am not willing to change myself for a   _____
relationship. Someone will love me de-
spite my looks.(C)

_____   I am willing to take as much time and   _____
spend as much money as it takes to find
the perfect relationship.(A)

_____   There are a number of things I like to   _____
do alone.(B)

_____   I hate doing anything alone.(C)   _____

_____   My after-work activities take up most of   _____
my spare time.(B)

_____   I wouldn't consider anyone who isn't in   _____
my own financial bracket.(C)

_____   It's important to me that my partner and   _____
I like to share the same activities and
sports.(B)

OVERALL EVALUATION SCORES:

Mini-questionnaire #1: _____
Mini-questionnaire #2: _____
Mini-questionnaire #3: _____
Mini-questionnaire #4: _____
Mini-questionnaire #5: _____

TOTAL: _____

If your score is 25 *or less,* you are not only ready but well on your way to finding love. I hope my book will act as a "refresher course," giving you some new ideas on how to meet a mate. Clearly, you are making love your first priority, and that's the way it's got to be. Your attitude is positive, and attitude is all-important. You may have to make some adjustments, do some fine-tuning, but . . . you're on your way!

If your score is *between 25 and 55 points,* you have a positive and open attitude toward finding love, but you now need to take the whole process a step further. Making love your first priority indicates serious commitment. I am going to help you take more definite and clear-cut steps toward finding love. The very first one is going to be establishing your priorities. After that, it's like dancing: when you know the steps perfectly, you can dance and enjoy the music without missing a beat.

All of you who scored 55 *points or above* need first to question whether or not you are really interested in *finding* love. Maybe you'd rather just dream about it? Maybe it's too much work? Maybe you actually like being alone? Or maybe a serious commitment is somehow threatening to you? But, if you're reading this book and you've taken the questionnaires, chances are you are serious about finding love but just don't quite know how to go about it. In that case, you've got your work cut out for you. I suggest you take each suggestion step-by-step. If, after reading it through, you decide that you are truly one of those people who have more important things in his/her life than finding love, don't feel bad. You're not alone. At some points in everyone's life, a job or career or study or travel may be the first priority. Remember, it's your privilege to be who you are. There's no law that says life is a Noah's Ark, that we all *must* go two-by-two every single step of the way!

Here's a helpful hint. Go back over your individual scores for each mini-questionnaire. See if there are some scores higher than the rest. This will provide you with important information about yourself. It will help you to pinpoint those areas of your life (self, family, finances, work, past experiences) that are holding you back from taking the necessary steps toward finding your love partner.

Examine the question "Do I really want a partner?" carefully. Look at those answers. If you find your mother, or family and friends, or peer pressure, or society lurking in the background, watch out! If your reasons don't represent the real you, it isn't going to work. Only a deep *wanting* is strong enough to pull "the real thing" into your life. If you don't have that, if you want to get married because your mother thinks you're living in sin, or is embarrassed to have an unmarried child over thirty (or twenty-five or whatever), think again. Remember, you have the right to take your time to find what's right for you. With the divorce rate what it is today, that's the only way to achieve something lasting and satisfying.

Look closely, too, at the question of *why* you want someone in your life. If it's because you feel "you're nothing without someone else," then get over that FAST or you'll project an insecure, unattractive image. You want somebody who's "something," don't you? Then doesn't it make sense for that person *also* to want somebody who thinks he or she is "something" too? Ditto if you're looking for a partner to rescue you from your own failings. If you can't balance your checkbook or do your own laundry or cooking, you may need a secretary or accountant, or a housekeeper or a maid. True, some mates do perform those functions for each other—but that's no good reason to go out looking for a life-partner. Or, perhaps you've discovered that really *working* at a relationship just doesn't appeal to you that much. The crucial thing here is to be honest with yourself. Sometimes we just *think* we want something, and suffer a lot from not having it. Or sometimes we want something for the wrong reasons.

Looking for the *right* reasons brings success. Think about it.

Is finding love your *first* priority? Let me tell you a story.

A year or so ago I had a phone call from a man who wanted my advice about finding love. Over that period of time he called me frequently, and he took my advice. Now, guess what happened?

Just a few weeks ago when he called me again, he was with a woman—he had found love, following the path I charted for him. You'd think this was a happy ending, wouldn't you? Unfortunately, there's a hitch. They'd ignored one piece of advice—the BIG ONE I'm talking to you about right now—I mean about love being your first priority. Here's what happened . . .

They met and wooed and loved, and they agreed that they were right for each other. The hitch? She's a bank president in Seattle and he's got a super job with a great future with an engineering firm in south Florida! What do they do?

Now, I'm well aware that jobs as bank presidents don't grow on trees (not in south Florida, and especially not for women) and he had already discovered that the engineering possibilities for him in Seattle and environs were the pits. How could I advise them? Simply. Either love *is* your first priority, or it *isn't*. There's just no in between. Something has to give. I can't tell her to quit her job in Seattle, or tell him to give up his opportunities in Florida. But if love is truly their first priority, they will find a way, even if it means both of them quitting their jobs and moving somewhere else and starting all over again.

Some people seem to think that you can have *two* first priorities at the same time—love and a career. I'm afraid it just isn't possible. Usually, of course, the situation doesn't become quite this serious, *but what if it does?* It's at this point that what your relationship means to you will be put to the test. And if the relationship isn't your absolutely *top* priority, it will suffer. It's as simple as that. Of course you have every right to choose your career over love, but, having done so, you *don't* have the right to complain about the "difficulty"—or "impossibility" (yes, I hear that too) of finding love.

Geography isn't the only problem. Even if two people are living in the same town, if one of them is a medical intern spending eighteen hours a day at the hospital, and that medical career is the top priority for that person, the love affair is going to suffer.

So again, check your priorities. In order to find and have a permanent mate, love must be the first item on everybody's agenda. Otherwise, you start talking about fitting love into a secondary slot—weekends, vacations, the "same time next year" syndrome, or a series of one-night stands with the same person. If having and loving and living with each other isn't your number one priority, then he stays with his job while she stays with hers, or one stays in one place and the other just visits. Any way you cut it, the relationship will probably end eventually.

Are you ready to go through the entire process with us to find love? Are you willing to make it your first priority—at least for a while? If so, read on . . .

Throughout the mini-questionnaires, we've scattered some key questions to indicate your willingness to make changes in your life in order to find love. It's not always easy to make those changes, but if you're not willing to make the necessary—*absolutely necessary*—effort, then *put down this book right now*. Go out and buy yourself a romance novel instead.

How much money and time are you willing to invest to find love? There's only one answer I'll accept: as much as necessary. Of course, few of us can spend unlimited amounts of money, but this is a serious business we're investing in. There's simply got to be some cash outlay involved here.

After all, we're talking about the person you are going to spend the rest of your life with. *You*. (Fooled you, didn't I? You thought I was going to say *him* or *her*.)

Which brings me to my next topic . . . know what the most powerful sex organ in the human body, male or female, is? Not what you think! I'm talking about the *brain*. Finding love is not going to be a random, hit-or-miss adventure. It requires *thought,* too. Most of us wouldn't dream of going about getting a job or running a business the way we go about the business of finding love. A lot of us put more thought into buying a new car than getting a life mate. So, be prepared to put your *brains* to work—in the service of your heart.

Later on we're going to go into detail about the reasons for past failures in your relationships. Unless we're talking about first love, you need to be aware of *why* other relationships have gone on the rocks. If there's an unfinished one lurking in the shadows, consciously or unconsciously (I call it the mooning-pining syndrome), or a load of guilts and insecurities, then make cleaning out your romantic closet your *first* order of business.

You also want to consider at the outset what kind of person is going to be right for you. Take another look at Mini-Questionnaire #3. Reread the questions. Think. Now sit down with pen and paper and make a list of those qualities you want in another person. Or *think* you want. Pay attention to the ones that are strictly you and put a big red X by the ones that belong to someone else—your mother, your father, family, friends, teachers, or anyone else who may, subtly or not-so-subtly, be influencing your life. Watch out for those old "parent tapes" that run in our heads . . . "Marry a doctor, a good provider," or "Be sure she knows how to cook and take care of you," or any of the others that get programmed into us along with our orange juice and vitamins, dance lessons and summers at camp.

After you finish your list and after you've weeded out what *you* want as opposed to what you're *supposed* to want, go off to a quiet, tranquil place and do some fantasizing. That's what I said. *Fantasy.* No, we're not going to suggest you dream up a lover—after all, we're talking *practicalities* here. But fantasy is an important part of our process. Imagine meeting your fantasy lover. Start a conversation. Go out on a date. Find out about his/her interests. Are they just like yours? Does it matter if they're not? How do you feel about having this person around all of the time, making concessions, perhaps compromising once in a while, maybe not always doing what *you* want? Does it feel good?

What's the reason for this exercise? Well, before you can achieve, you must perceive. If your fantasy is wildly unrealistic (did you imagine Richard Gere or Raquel Welch?), then go back and check your list. Maybe you'd better make a list of your own qualities, and include the ones you don't like so much right along with your sparkling points. Do the two lists mesh, or at least seem compatible? If not, better readjust that fantasy.

I want you now to consider carefully just how you spend your everyday time—not vacations, not special occasions, not your duty dinner with the folks. *Your* time. This is important, because if two people disagree on how to spend their time together (and apart), it's almost as disastrous as disagreeing about how to spend money. And most people never bother to analyze how they spend their time. It just goes (like some people's money "just goes"). Especially today, when both partners in a love relationship are likely to be working at full-time jobs, this is critical. If your idea of a great time is four hours a night glued to the TV and your partner's is going out on the town, it might not be terrific for long, no matter how sexually or conversationally happy you might be. If your twice-weekly dance lesson or gym class means a lot, and you tend to get aggressive and nervous without your regular exercise, you might not be very content with a partner whose idea of exercise is reaching for the telephone. The trick is striving for balance. As long as you *know* what's important to you, you can slot it in. It's being *aware* that counts.

As you make your list and go over the answers to the questionnaires, you'll begin to get a pretty clear picture of your "personal profile." If you're not particularly happy with the picture, don't worry about it! I'm going to help you do something about it.

While we're on the subject of self-analysis, I'd like to bring up cultural attitudes. This is a crucial part of your own reality profile. For example, is religion important to your choice of a partner? Make sure this value is appropriate to the way you live now. If you're carrying around a belief left over from childhood which has no particular relevance to the way you live now, then this contingency regarding the cultural attitudes of your future mate may be unnecessarily limiting.

Take Millie. A bright, pretty and successful woman in her thirties, she is from an Italian Catholic background (though she doesn't practice), and she is looking for a husband. She decided to run an ad in the personal columns of her city's magazine. Out of the answers, she picked several to get in touch with. One of them, a neurosurgeon, was named Charles. After a pleasant conversation with him, she was ready to have a date with him . . . until she heard his last name. Charles was Chinese, and she refused to even see him.

What if she'd fallen in love with him? She wants a husband and children, and though she doesn't insist on a Catholic man, she does not want to risk any cross-cultural relationships. It seems silly to me. I have an American friend who is happily married to a Chinese man. Except for his Chinese name, he is an American and as Christian as his wife. Their children are beautiful. This family hasn't suffered one bit from its cross-cultural mixing. In fact, it's been enhanced.

Now, I'm not suggesting that everybody go out and marry someone of a different race, but I am saying that if you deliberately limit your opportunities to meet and greet people you certainly do narrow your chances for finding love! Of course, if staying within your own cultural confines is of the utmost importance to you, you have to act accordingly. But who's to say that Millie's unmet Chinese friend might not have enriched her life, introduced her to new experiences, or even introduced her to a Caucasian man to fall in love with!

Don't let your cultural attitudes *unnecessarily* limit your chances at romance.

Knowing yourself is the way to take control of your ability to find love. If you leave the business of finding love to chance, chances are it'll pass you right by.

2

Get Set

HAVE YOU EVER wondered *why* a handsome guy is talking to a pretty woman at a bar, when his attitude plainly says, "Stay away"?

He's distracted. Opportunity for love has "knocked," but he can't concentrate because he's thinking about his collar (it's smudged), his shoes (boy, do they need a shine), and he's sure that there's this murky odor coming from him.

He doesn't even hear what she's saying. How could he? He's too busy asking himself why he didn't bother to go home, shower, and change clothes before he went out.

He's so preoccupied with the impression he's making that he can't relax, and his companion is getting the message that he doesn't want her to get too close.

Sound familiar?

SALLY'S BASIC RULE

Don't go anywhere—repeat anywhere—unless you're looking good. Not even to the supermarket or the laundromat. This is one way to make sure you will be ready when the opportunity for love presents itself. You never know who will be waiting around the next corner!

Take Susie from Kansas City. She was *sure* she'd never find love. But after we talked, she spruced up her appearance. Even if she was only going out for a quart of milk, she made sure she looked good.

One Saturday morning while doing errands, she met Dick, who was new to the neighborhood. With her hair combed, wearing makeup, instead of wanting to crawl into the nearest hole, she had the confidence to suggest showing him the area. He invited her for coffee. They exchanged phone numbers. A few days later, he asked her to a party his brother Dan was giving. Though Susie had liked Dick, she found Dan delightful. The feeling was mutual. A week later Susie and Dan were a twosome. Susie's found love. But what if she'd been unsure and unconfident about her appearance that Saturday morning? What if she had gone out shopping with no makeup and wearing sloppy clothes?

But being neat and clean isn't everything. Whether we like it or not (and I don't, but we'll get into that later), ours is a society of *packaging*. As much as each one of us would like to—and deserve to—be taken on our *merits*, there's just too much media manipulation going on for that to work.

So let's deal with it. You are going to have to "package" yourself to get what you want.

Is this necessarily bad? No, it isn't. It's just smart—and *practical*. Whether you are a man or a woman, your appearance is going to be the first impression you make. And that doesn't mean just the way you comb your hair or dress. It's how you walk, how you stand, how you smile (or *if* you do!). It's the general impression you create before you even open your mouth. (*After* you open your mouth is another story!) To use an old saying, it's the whole nine yards.

What we're talking about here is the entire process of

finding love. It's not just an act or series of acts. It is a process of *self-transformation*. That word *self* is important, especially if you're suffering from any insecurities (who isn't?). There's a beginning, a middle, and an end to this process. A happy end. Remember, though, that everything is based on the current priority in your life.

The first thing, the absolutely first thing, is to get your*self* together. Not only for that possibly all-important person who is a prospect for love, but for *you*. How you look tells the world how you feel about yourself. Consider that for a moment.

There's not a one of us alive who hasn't at some time or other been in despair about our looks. Perhaps it was because we "just couldn't do a thing with" our hair, or had a blemish on our skin, or "felt fat," or because our favorite and most flattering dress or suit was at the cleaner's when an unexpected invitation came up. All of us have at one time or another turned down an invitation to a party because we just didn't feel our appearance was up to snuff, or gone to the party feeling hopelessly unattractive, thereby *guaranteeing* a miserable time.

First, let's take our bodies. Almost all of us, with the possible exception of models, dancers, and professional athletes, could use *some* tuning up. It's not easy. I know that. You'd be surprised to find that it becomes a lot easier when you have a good reason for doing it. And what better reason than your own health and happiness? Your *self*?

Let's talk for a moment about health. I'm all for the physical fitness movement in this country—it couldn't have come at a better time, with all the junk food we consume and the hours we spend *sitting* in front of the television. But it *has* been carried too far by some, and you surely don't have to swallow 400 vitamin pills and run 33 miles a day to be healthy and fit.

What about the wonderful glow that comes from just being a healthy human being? You can't change genes, so there's no point in wishing for Elizabeth Taylor's violet eyes or Tom Selleck's body, but you can make the most of what you've got—the healthy way.

Being healthy has other benefits, too. It means vitality, that indispensable quality of being rarin' to go, of being ready and able to shape our experience.

You are your own work of art—physically, mentally, and spiritually, and it's up to you to create an attractive portrait. Unfortunately, all too often, you're too unsure of yourself and you wonder . . . where do I begin? Well, listen: most people are insecure, and a lot of that insecurity comes from just not feeling quite up to par. I'm going to say it again: you have only one body. Take care of it.

Your whole life works better if your machinery works. This is not to say you have to try to emulate the too-perfect people you see on TV, in the movies, and in the magazines. In fact, quite the opposite is true. You only have to get to be the best *you* can be. You've got to look at yourself and say, "Okay, this is what I've got to work with. Is this the best *me?* Where do I go from here?"

You don't have to make any radical changes (though we won't rule them out if they are necessary). You don't have to suddenly play a smashing game of tennis. What you do have to do is sculpt out the best you from the material at hand—your body and your attitude toward it.

Let me give you an example from real life. My friend Jack was looking for a girlfriend. He signed up with one of the dating services, a pricey one at that. They gave him some names and he looked over the resumes of the women and was intrigued. He made a date with Darlene, a long-stemmed dark beauty. Being a chivalrous kind of guy, and a food and wine critic as well, he invited her out to a fabulous restaurant for dinner. Not a bad start, right?

Wrong! A disastrous start. Jack and Darlene never got past go. Poor Darlene was allergic to such a wide variety of common foods—onions, garlic, and so on—that she could barely eat. Her gastronomic frailty was not exactly an aphrodisiac for poor Jack, and I can tell you that he's not alone. Most men love to see a woman enjoy her food.

Needless to say, Jack didn't ask Darlene for a second date after watching her pick through dinner like a soldier treading over a mine field. Of course, there may not be much Darlene can do about her allergies, but my point is that nobody wants a partner who is consistently under par, whatever the cause. And there *are* ways to minimize health problems. I have a friend who has chronic low-back pain. Instead of complaining, or letting it spoil her active life, she goes to a chiropractor once a week, and, while her life's not pain-free, she takes the best care of herself she can and makes sure she gets extra rest if she has a heavy schedule.

So, what could Darlene have done prior to setting out on *her* quest for love? (She'd paid too for the pricey dating service.) She could have asked a doctor or nutritionist about the various treatments available for her food allergies. Then she could adapt more easily to dining out—one of the bulwarks of our social structure.

In most cases, there are just too many new techniques available today—including those of natural healing and nutrition—for anyone to suffer excessively or needlessly.

How to get yourself into as healthy a state as possible for who and what you are right now? Well, you can be ten pounds overweight and still be extremely healthy. Remember, we are not discussing some unattainable state of physical perfection or movie-star-quality beauty. We're talking about *you*. The you that *you* are right now and the *you* that you are capable of becoming with a bit of effort.

The key word here is discipline. This discipline comes, not from setting and keeping to a rigid schedule, but from knowing always that, no matter what, you can put your best foot forward. If you need to lose some pounds, don't think of it as a grind of "giving up" your favorite pastime.

Think instead of the rewards of feeling good, of new energy, of new attractiveness.

Exercise. It doesn't have to be a drag. There's a form of activity for everyone—and the easiest and most natural is simply *walking*. You don't have to join a health club or become a marathon runner to bring healthful activity into your life. Once you can see the positive value of improving your physical self to achieve your goals (and remember, you're the one setting the priorities!), it will become easier. That's a *promise*.

One thing that I observe time and time again is that most people are looking for what's *comfortable*. All you have to do is turn on the radio, watch TV, go to the movies, or read a magazine to see that whether it's Michelob-your-weekend or double-strength aspirin, the accent is on *not* feeling the pain. The outcome of this implicit message that "feeling good is being good" (and I won't go into my feelings about the emotional immaturity it represents) is the tremendous dependence on drugs and alcohol that we see in our society.

In terms of finding love, this laziness has perpetuated the fantasy that one day we are going to run into somebody who will love us for what we are. So why should we change one iota of our present selves when eventually we will be discovered and loved without having to work? Well, if that's *your* attitude, you don't need this book. Maybe it will happen to you that way. And maybe it won't. But I'm talking about making changes, and if you're not willing to look beyond your living room, or take a good, hard, *honest* look at yourself, then you won't profit from my advice.

Do you know the difference between fairy tale and reality? Between hoping it will happen and working for it? I want to hear an unqualified yes to that question. Because that's what's going to take us to the READY stage. Either you're ready to make the changes because it's important enough to you to do so, or you aren't. If you were in school and told you were failing and would be kicked out if you didn't get your grades up, you'd hit the books, wouldn't you? Or if you were in business and your accountant advised you to cut back on your expenses or you'd go bankrupt, you'd heed his advice, wouldn't you? Why would you want to conduct love with any less effort and imagination?

I'm going to divide the problem of getting ready to find love into four parts: physical health, emotional health, attitudes, and social confidences. Remember that in the end it all hooks together to be *you*.

I've mentioned insecurities. There is a cure for them, and it's called *confidence*. Let's talk about physical confidence. This means, quite simply, feeling good about your body and having the confidence to use it—whether for sports or sex, work or play, eating or sleeping.

It might seem that there's not much more to be said on this matter, but a closer look will show it to be quite a complex topic. There's no question about it: your level of body confidence affects the rest of you. The more you have, the better you're going to like yourself, the more attractive a self you're going to project to others, especially in new or different situations.

Take an ordinary situation. You go out, feeling frisky. This morning you stepped on the scale and noticed that you'd lost a couple of pounds. You feel lighter, more confident. Maybe your belt is a notch tighter. There's a smile on your face. The sun seems to be shining just for you. Your walk is tall, your stride long. Even to passersby you are communicating a whole lot about yourself and how you feel about yourself. People smile back. That's body confidence at work.

You might not like my next suggestion, but just like in those good old "golden rule" days, you're going to find the public library a tool in your quest for love. And, no, I don't mean as a place to meet prospective lovers (though I wouldn't rule out the possibility). Books are what I'm recommending—and today there are dozens of books available on physical fitness, shaping up, bodywork, diets from A to Z. Every magazine published seems to come up with a new diet each month. I won't tell you what's going to work for you, but I will suggest that you take a look and decide for yourself. Don't look only at the books published in the past year. Check out the old standards as well. Records, too, are available from your library. Your television also offers you programming designed to help you get into shape. And today you can get videos for just about any exercise program that you can imagine; programs for the young and vigorous or the middle-aged and cautious; from the super-strenuous to those designed for the beginner or more out of shape. Whether you want to study relaxation or yoga, aerobics or dance, there are video programs available to suit every taste, each individual need. Do some research, find a plan that appeals to you, and get to work.

Maybe your body is just fine. Trim and shapely, not a spare ounce, firm where it should be, strong, healthy. Ah, but that face! Not the one that launched a thousand ships, you think. There's a little poem by a well-known humorist that goes: "As a beauty I'm not a great star, but my face, I don't mind it, for I am behind it. It's the people out front that I jar."

If that's your feeling about your face, then this is the area of your body for you to concentrate on. Here's my advice: *If there's something you don't like, do something about it*. I am totally in favor of cosmetic surgery. Physical problems can seriously affect our emotions. We think of them as defects. Cosmetic is a deceptively—and unfairly—frivolous word for something so important that it can mar a person's confidence from childhood onward. The fact that many insurance plans haven't caught on and still consider corrective surgery for non-illness conditions to be "unnecessary" and therefore uncovered, is a great pity. That may mean you're going to have to shell out your own hard-earned money for the medical expenses. But don't complain. Remember when I asked you how much money you are willing to invest to find love—and I said that the only possible answer was *whatever is necessary?*

Just look at that *nose,* you might be thinking as you zip into your chic new jumpsuit. Who's going to love that thing? If you've been fixated on your nose for ages, make plans to change it. Find out what kind of doctor you need to solve the problem. Many of these—such as frown lines or weak chins—can be corrected by simple office procedures. Many's the man with a "weak" chin and a passive, mild-mannered disposition who has turned into a roaring tiger with the addition of a nice, firm, manly chin. I do not joke. On the other hand, I am not suggesting you tamper with a perfectly nice nose in a reach toward some unattainable standard of beauty.

Make sure you get the *best* advice you can. Friends and relatives are fine, and they love you. Love, however, is not known for its objectivity. Professionals are. That's why they get paid. After you've gotten advice and considered it seriously in the light of all of your alternatives, *act.*

This goes for *anything* that bothers you, whether you are going bald and you hate it (get a transplant), have varicose or spider veins (easily removed in the doctor's office), have skin problems (see the dermatologist), have bags under your eyes (a simple operation these days), are embarrassed by your glasses (check out contacts), or need your teeth straightened (adults of any age can have teeth fixed today).

That trip to the dentist is also all-important. Your teeth are not only a major part of your general health, they are usually the front runner when you meet a new person. I mean your smile. If you're afraid to smile, or if you cover your mouth with your hand while you talk, it's bound to detract more than a little bit from your overall impression. Another thing about teeth is that they should be *clean*—not just your usual regular brushing, but the kind of professional cleaning only a dentist's hygienist can give you. And while you're at it, don't forget to have your dentist check your smile. Perhaps you have minor problems of discoloration or unevenness; ask you dentist about a procedure called *bonding*. It's easy, relatively inexpensive compared to caps, and effective. For the best smile in town—one that is *confident*—you need not only good teeth but relaxed facial muscles, especially the jaws. Tension produces a tight, unhappy smile. There are special exercises to correct this, and, done a few times each day, they will give you a relaxed, happy smile.

Let's say you have a feature or problem that's been bugging you for years, and now you're ready to do something about it. Before you take action, make sure you really *do* have a problem, that you're not just imagining your looks won't do. A call I had from a young fellow called Hank will demonstrate what I mean.

HANK: Hello, Sally. I want to say four words before I get into my problem: Please help. I'm desperate.

SJR: All right, tell me your problem.

HANK: . . . It's about girls. Since I'm visually handicapped the girls don't want to be around me. I'm not too much of a good-looking guy.

SJR: How do you know?

HANK: I've looked in the mirror.

SJR: Oh, so you're not that visually handicapped.

HANK: (He laughs.) Well, I'm not blind.

SJR: Maybe you're nearsighted if you think you're not good looking.

HANK: Well, I've been turned down (for dates) so much.

SJR: And you really think it's your looks? If you do, there are things you can do. But why don't you ask other people what you look like?

HANK: 'Cause it's hard when you're eighteen to know what you look like. At eighteen when things aren't going well, we blame it on our looks.

SJR: Aren't there guys who aren't as good looking as you doing all right? Isn't Dudley Moore doing all right?

HANK: Yeah.

SJR: Is he as good looking as you?

HANK: He's a little homely, if you ask me.

SJR: OK. We could go on with a long list of people, but you know what they do have: they have a real sense of self-confidence; they think they're good looking . . . and that's what it really takes.

If you're not too sure what needs improvement, make a short checklist:

Face		*Body*
Hair (see Chapter 6)	Lips	Excess hair
Teeth	Skin	Warts or moles
Chin	Eyes	Surface cysts
Nose	Ears	Foot problems (keep
Makeup (for both	Facial hair	you inactive)
men and women)		Any chronic pain
or grooming aids		(makes you tense)

Ask a friend—not a close friend, but someone you know well enough to trust, but not *too* well (*not* your mother, probably not family, unless it's a brother- or sister-in-law)—to help you take stock. Ask, "Is my nose too big?" or "Should I have my teeth straightened?" or "Would an eye job help?" or "Do my veins show that badly?" or "Are my ears too big, or do they stick out too much?" If your friends assure you that you're perfectly fine just as you are, but your gut tells you differently, go with your gut.

Now I'm going to tell you a story, that will address the emotional and the mental aspects of getting ready to find love.

Frances is a fifty-one-year-old woman, very bright, a successful career counselor, with two lovely grown daughters. Twice married (once divorced, once widowed) with a goodly number of affairs in between, you'd think she would have fairly high confidence about her looks, wouldn't you? Well, you'd be dead wrong. Even though every time Fran goes on vacation (which she does frequently, often to exotic spots), she comes home with yet another tale of *amour* she found, she's *never* even felt pretty! Not exactly ugly, just not pretty. She always thought the men who liked her had bad eyesight, or maybe bad judgment. One day, she and some of her colleagues were playing a fantasy game. It went like this: if you could have anything in the world you wanted for *one day only,* what would it be?

While the others were spinning out their fantasies (one fellow wanted to meet *all* of the Playgirls, for example), Fran thought about it. When her turn came, she surprised everyone—including herself.

"I'd like, just for once, to look so absolutely smashing that when I walked by heads would turn to look at me."

At that point something long buried clicked inside Fran. She heard her own words, heard her own longing for a better (and *obtainable*) her. While I'm not going to explore the psychological problems that may have prompted Fran's insecurity, I'd like to mention here that some people do have deep-seated psychological problems connected to their looks, and for those people some sort of psychotherapy might be warranted (again: get professional advice). Sometimes corrective surgery alone isn't enough to heal the inside person. Sometimes the person who has the surgery goes on seeing what was there before. Therapy can help both in making the decision to have the surgery and in accepting those changes as part of the real you once they are accomplished.

Let me turn from Fran for a moment to give you a brief example of what turned out to be a psychological problem resulting from corrective surgery.

Lila had a nose that was not only extremely large for her petite face and features, it was really *ugly*. Other than that huge nose, she was—or could have been—quite pretty, but the size and shape of her nose amounted to a deformity. And that was just how Lila felt—deformed. Her parents were aware of the pain this caused her all through her adolescence but, because she was still growing, nothing could be done until she was eighteen and ready for college.

Then, as a graduation present, her parents gave her the plastic surgery. *Voila!* A beautiful new nose, revealing a very pretty face. Life went on and Lila had plenty of boyfriends and a happy social life all through college and her first working years. Then she married. She'd never told her husband about the ''nose job.'' She had more or less forgotten it herself, or so she thought.

When Lila became pregnant a couple of years into the marriage, both she and her husband were delighted. But as Lila's baby girl grew up, it quickly became clear that the little daughter was a carbon copy of her mother, with the old nose. Lila fell into a deep depression. She hated the ''old'' self that she saw in her child. Her husband thought the baby was cute as could be, but Lila couldn't be consoled. Guilt raised its ugly head. It was her fault the child had her nose.

Psychotherapy helped Lila to accept her baby as a whole person, not as someone deformed. And now she is prepared to help her child with building up her self-image in a positive and caring way until the baby is old enough to get a new nose.

I understand how seriously we all feel about our looks,

and I don't for a moment want you to think of yourself as "vain" or frivolous for having or considering cosmetic surgery. Those pangs we suffer are real, just as real as— and sometimes more painful than—physical pain.

But let's go back to Fran. She, too, had had some years of therapy, which paved the way for her new recognition of herself. The re-creating of the self is not an overnight process. Here's what she did and what she now says about the experience.

What had bothered her all these years were her buck teeth or, to put it more kindly, a prominent protrusion of the upper plate. She'd learned to live with it, more or less. After some periodontal and orthodontal work, she discovered she had no chin! What she had been blaming on her teeth (though they were partly at fault) had really been the lack of chin.

For the first time she imagined her face the way she wanted it to be. She realized that a new chin would round off the new picture she was creating out of her old self. Remember what I said about you being your own work of art? Well, Fran went for a chin implant, a procedure that took two short sessions in the doctor's office, a week apart.

Sporting her new face—and *loaded with confidence*— she went out and bought a new wardrobe. Then, when her old car broke down, she agonized for a couple of weeks about the expense of the repairs and the anxiety of another breakdown. Finally, getting dressed for work one morning in a new outfit, with her hair freshly done to show off her "new" face, she decided that such a smashing-looking person deserved a *new* car.

Yep. You guessed it. She went out and bought herself a new car! True, she couldn't really afford it, but she didn't have any trouble convincing the bank that they wanted to finance it. Not when she breezed into the loan officer's presence with her new self-confidence.

Do *you* ever wonder what you would look like if your ears were flatter? Your nose smaller? There are numerous ways to find a specialist in your area. You can contact the American Society of Plastic and Reconstructive Surgeons, or you can ask your own doctor for a recommendation. You can call or write to the plastic surgery department of the nearest large hospital, preferably a teaching hospital. Ask for the names of three surgeons so that you can get more than one opinion. If you know someone, or know someone who knows someone, who has had *successful* plastic surgery, ask that person to recommend his or her physician. But *do* get more than one opinion.

Are you ready to GET SET to find love? You have to put your best foot—and best face and body—forth at all times, under all circumstances. (If you get caught in a mudslide in California, of course, I'll excuse you—but only for the moment.)

You must be ready and willing to make the effort to make the necessary changes in the way you present yourself to all those prospective mates out there. You need to take an analytical, objective look at yourself—not only to spot the flaws and do something about them, but to understand the *great* things about yourself and make the most of them. If you've got gorgeous eyes, learn to *use* them! Flirt!

Read on.

Procedure	Cases Per Year	Range of Fees*
1. Breast augmentation (enlargement)	72,000	$1,000–2,000
2. Blepharoplasty (eyelid surgery)	56,500	$1,000–1,500
3. Rhinoplasty (nose reshaping)	54,000	$1,200–1,800

4. Rhytidectomy (face lift)	39,000	$2,000–3,000
5. Breast reduction	32,000	$2,000–2,500
6. Dermabrasion (acne scar/wrinkle removal)	17,000	$ 500–1,000
7. Abdominoplasty (tightening of hanging abdomen)	15,300	$1,500–2,500
8. Mastopexy (breast raising)	12,800	$1,500–2,500
9. Otoplasty (ear reshaping)	11,500	$ 800–1,200
10. Liposuction (fat removal)	4,000	$1,500–3,000

Other procedures you might want to look into: Liposuction is especially good for knees and upper arms, and it can often be done in the doctor's office. Other procedures you might investigate are silicon and collagen implants (silicon is permanent; collagen is "fugitive," which means that the implant can move about under your skin), which are good for pock-marks, labial lines, crow's feet, and other imperfections. For balding there's now Minoxidil. (Check with your physician for a prescription.)

*The range of fees quoted above may change due to inflation. Check with a reliable plastic surgeon if you are considering a procedure. Or you can call the American Association of Plastic Surgeons in your city for information and the names of doctors. It is always wise to get a second opinion for any surgical prodecure, and don't be embarrassed to shop around for prices. With plastic surgery becoming ever more popular for cosmetic purposes, clinics are springing up all over and they are highly competitive. This does not mean cheapest is best, but the most expensive need not be necessary either. Feel free to discuss any details and ask questions of any doctor you are considering to work on your body. After all, it's your body or face and you want the very best for it.

3

Get Ready

"LOVE WALKED BY and where was I?" asks an old song. Where were *you?* Were you sending out signals telling people to keep away?

Take that fellow over there, leaning back in his chair with his arms firmly crossed over his manly chest. What do you think he's doing? What kind of signal is he sending out?

He may think he looks relaxed and eager for conversation but his body language is saying that he doesn't want anyone to come too close. He's busy protecting that vulnerable heart of his.

And look at the girl over there, with her hair pulled back in a tight bun and her arms held rigidly by her sides. She's smiling all right, but her body is saying that she's scared to experience her sensual feelings. Even if she's not aware of it, she's wearing a "don't touch" sign, and others will probably follow the unspoken directions.

One day I was in a ladies' room, standing in front of a mirror, when a much older, more glamorous woman came up beside me and proceeded to tell me all about her date, her life—everything. I stood there combing my hair and listening and nodding, wondering why she had picked *me* to confide in. Then she said, "You know, I feel a lot better now that I've talked to you," and smiling, picked up her purse and left.

Afterward, I wondered aloud—and to myself—why she had talked to me. I wasn't the only other lady in the ladies' room. It occurred to me that her response to me had to have something to do with the way I *looked*. She certainly didn't know *who* I was. There must have been something about my body language that told the woman in the bathroom I would be receptive to her story.

What about your body language? The first thing that you need to know about it, in relation to finding love, is that much of it is probably totally unconscious. There *are* books you can read on the subject—some good, some not so good, written mostly by anthropologists who study the behavior of gorillas, mute swans (who, incidentally, mate for life and should therefore make interesting subject matter, or at least serve as a good example for humans), wolf spiders, and the like.

There's a lot to study on nonverbal communication nowadays. If you're really interested, by all means get some books and learn what you can.

First off, what you need to know is that there is an *internal* you running the show that the outside world is watching. If you want an example of what I'm talking about in living color, just have a nice chat on the phone with a friend (preferably one of the opposite sex) while sitting in front of a mirror.

Watch not only your facial expressions, but watch what you do with your body. Do you gesture with your hands or keep them still? Do you fidget, twirl a strand of your hair in your fingers or stroke your beard or mustache? Do you slump or sit straight? Is the general attitude of your body rigid or is it relaxed? How conscious are you of how you look and what you're doing?

The search for love is affected by the messages that we give out and receive. It's not only necessary to know what we're sending, it's equally important to know how to interpret what we're receiving. This doesn't mean you have to become an anthropologist and go study swans. It means you need to become *aware*.

Becoming aware of your own body, evaluating its assets, flaws, needs, as we have discussed, will help make you aware of how *you* signal and how other people signal you. Love itself might seem an intangible commodity, but the signals we use to look for it are very real indeed.

Let me give you an example.

A man goes to a crowded function, say a meeting of his business association. It's an after-work cocktail party in a big hotel. If he's taken my advice, he's already spruced himself up a bit, maybe shaved and splashed on a bit of the newest men's cologne. He wanders about rather aimlessly for a while, mildly bored by the whole affair. With the ice melting in his drink, he says hello to the Jacks and Jills he knows from his working environment and is wondering how soon he can decently leave.

Then he spots a woman across the room. Yes, across a crowded room. It *does* happen. There is something about the way she is standing, chatting to a couple of people, that attracts him. Suddenly his whole posture changes. He stands straighter, his hand goes to his tie to check if it's straight, he glances quickly and maybe furtively at his reflection in the glass-paneled window. He moves toward the room, and now his walk is somehow different from when he was merely doing his duty.

When he finally reaches the woman, she is now standing alone, looking quite content with herself. Her eyes are not darting about the room for a companion. She doesn't fidget. A small smile plays around her lips. Keeping in mind the excuses that this is a business affair, he easily goes up and introduces himself.

"I'm John Smith," he says, extending his hand politely. "Acme Corporation."

"Marsha Davis," she says, taking his hand and giving it a firm, *not limp*, handshake. "Davis Associates. Nice to meet you." As she speaks, she looks directly into his eyes.

"Can I get you a new drink?" he asks, looking down at the melting ice she's holding. "Yours looks as sad as mine."

"Yes, that would be nice," she replies, smiling and handing him her glass.

He takes it but doesn't at first move away. She shifts her purse to her shoulder so that both hands are free. Her arms hang loosely by her sides, relaxed. He is holding the two glasses and facing her.

"What are you drinking?" he asks, turning slightly toward the bar and seeming to survey the path he is going to forge through the mass of people to do the lady a service.

"Scotch and soda," she says, her eyes conveying the message that she likes the way he looks and appreciates his polite attitude.

Off he goes, plunging through the crowd like a knight in shining armor. She watches, an expression of keen interest knitting her pretty brow. He moves like a man with a mission—politely cutting through the crowd, not shoving, not being rude, but getting to the bar in record time.

He returns and hands her the fresh drink, a bit disheveled from the effort, a strand of hair looped over his forehead.

"Thanks," she says, smiling more widely, almost a small laugh. She *looks* as if she might be about to laugh.

"That was hard work," she says and reaches up and gently puts the lock of hair back in place. It is *not* a caress, it is a small service. He has done her one by getting the drink, she returns it by tidying him up.

"This place is jammed," he says ruefully. "Where did all these people come from?"

It's a rhetorical question and he doesn't expect an answer.

"Out of the woodwork," she says, fishing into her purse for a cigarette, her head tilted slightly toward him, for she has hung her purse on the arm near to him. "There weren't this many last month."

He lights her cigarette, moving a step closer.

With virtually no conversation of any importance, these two people already know quite a bit about each other. They also know that they are attracted and are deciding underneath the banter what to do about it. She knows that he is direct and forceful, but also polite and considerate. He knows that she can handle herself competently alone, but that she is open and warm to new acquaintances. Usually we attract the opposite sex *unconsciously* from an inner self that dictates our unspoken actions. Just as these nonverbal signals are instinctive for each of us, they are often registered by others unconsciously. The man wasn't thinking, "Oh, she's warm and friendly and I'd like to get to know her"; he was *responding* from the gut level, and that response propelled him across the room to fetch her that drink.

She wasn't thinking, "He's direct and forceful and kind and considerate." She was absorbing his atmosphere and responding to it by her positive acceptance of his offer.

Later, on reflection, each may think about how they learned what they learned, but the process happens too fast for on-the-spot evaluation. It is automatic. And this is why a high level of awareness is needed. As in driving a car, one's reflexive actions must be in tune at all times. Just as you never know when an accident will happen, you never know when an opportunity for love will present itself. Have you gotten the point yet? *You have to be ready at all times*. And it can't be said often enough: the more aware you are of yourself, the more free you are to be yourself, and the more free you feel, the more natural you'll be. The more natural you are, the more you open yourself up to receive impressions from others and respond positively to them. Lack of self-awareness, focusing on what you hate about yourself *(never* a fair evaluation) or your fears of how others perceive you, lead only to *self-consciousness,* not *self-confidence.* It's only when you reach a high level of self-awareness that you can let it go and *forget about yourself,* letting the true you shine through your actions.

Let's look at this little scene another way. Suppose the woman had been standing there chewing on her lip, tapping her foot, looking about her with an air of desperation, unable to be comfortable with standing alone with no one to talk to. Suppose the man had been rumpled, too rushed to care what he looked like, planning only to have a quick drink and cut out. Suppose further that when he approached the woman he hadn't offered to shake hands or get her a drink, but just hung there like an old suit of clothes on a hanger. You get the picture. Nothing much would have happened even if they did manage to strike up some sort of desultory shoptalk.

So, we're back to how you feel about yourself is going to affect how others feel about you. We've talked about the physical changes you can make, and about how these can affect your feelings about yourself and your receptivity to others. Now let's look at some helpful shifts in attitude that you can make—because even if the body is in tiptop shape, if the mind is not cooperating, you're not going to get very far.

I want to talk about one of the most common failings. It is giving off vibrations of *desperation.* And don't think only women do it. Men are just as prone to this disease as women. I'll tell you right now that there's no known cure. You can't take a pill for it and vitamins won't help.

What will help—the *only* thing that will help—is mental readjustment. Attitudes. After years of living with yourself, you'd think you'd know yourself pretty well, wouldn't you? Usually, nothing could be further from the truth. First, we are our own worst critics. In a study of young schoolgirls, three-quarters considered themselves to be the most *unattractive* girl in the class! Now, seventy-five percent of a class of girls cannot possibly all be at the bottom, can they? Yet, these young girls were being totally honest in their self-evaluations. Honest, but dead wrong. That's what I mean about attitudes.

If you've got a mental image of yourself that is holding you back from finding love, then I'm here to help you change it. We're going to cover those childhood bogies that so many of us are still living with later (whether we know it or not), but for now let's just take a quick look at your mental image of yourself.

Here's a quick checklist:

( ) I'm fat (or too thin).
( ) I'm just right as I am.
( ) I'm ugly (or plain, or unattractive).
( ) I'm quite attractive.
( ) I'm not the prettiest (or most handsome) but I think I'm fine as I am.
( ) I feel like a loser.
( ) I feel like a winner most of the time.
( ) I don't know how I feel. I'm confused.
( ) Most people I meet like me right off.
( ) It takes a while for people to warm up to me.
( ) People don't like me. What's the use?
( ) I was considered the "smart one," or "the pretty one," or the "athletic one," or any other "one" in my family.
( ) My sister or brother was considered the "_____one." (Fill in the blank and compare yourself.)
( ) My parents often complimented me about my looks or my abilities.

( ) I was always told that I was dumb, or unattractive, or
   incompetent.

There's no score to this little quiz. It's designed to help
you start some serious thinking about "where you're coming from" in terms of how you feel about yourself.

Unfortunately, those old childhood evaluations—from
parents or peers—can become self-fulfilling prophesies,
and all too frequently they do. I've often heard, "I was a
fat child. Everybody told me I was fat. That's why I'm fat
now." Even if the child who was suffering from malnutri-
tion was told he/she was fat, it's likely to become true.
What we need to do is rewind those old parent tapes and
rerecord *over* them our own positive image. How to arrive
at this new image? By objective evaluation and, yes,
awareness.

Here's where a friend can help. A lot of people simply
don't think to ask a friend about the way they are present-
ing themselves. Oh, we solicit opinions on the new dress
or suit, the new hairdo or shoes, but rarely do we ask
about how we *act*. We live in a society where social
politeness is expected and truthfulness, if it comes in the
form of something we would prefer not to hear, is considered rude. It's not fair to *expect* a friend to volunteer
information that might upset you, but by asking you give
permission for the person to be truthful, and you can
promise in advance not to have hurt feelings if you don't
like what's said.

However, a word of warning. Don't ask anyone who
might have a stored-up resentment or grudge against you.
That would be like taking the lid off the box. You need
objectivity and fairness, so ask a person who can be
trusted to be fair. Don't ask anyone with whom you have a
long-term, heavily invested emotional life, like your mother
or sister. Choose a person once-removed, perhaps your
best friend's wife or husband, even a colleague with whom

you have shared some experiences, who's seen you functioning around people. These traits are usually visible even in an office setting.

Another thing is a camera, although of course a photograph is two-dimensional. But if you hate looking at pictures of yourself, analyze *why*. Is it because of a grim look on your face? Do you think you look awkward? Again, ask someone else's opinion. A lot of us hate pictures of ourselves, those embarrassing candid shots, on principle. Get a friend to shoot a roll of photos of you in action and then give it to you to be developed. No one but *you* need see the results. Some people may feel a little shy or silly about studying pictures of themselves, but it's *okay*. You're not being narcissistic—you're being realistic. You can do it in complete privacy. It's a useful tool for getting a handle on your own appearance and how you'd like to improve it. To paraphrase the poet, we need to be able to see ourselves as others see us.

Make a speech in front of a mirror. Sure, you will be self-conscious at first, but the more you practice the easier it will become. Make a little scenario for yourself and act it out, playing both parts. Take an acting class or a dance class where there are mirrors on the wall. If you know a video nut, you could even try a videotape of yourself in action, but it ought to be some sort of action not planned for the camera. Later on you might want to join one of those videodating services (we'll be discussing dating services later) and this could be a sort of rehearsal.

Once you've collected some opinions, think about them. Begin to change slowly. If you fidget by twirling a curl or tweaking your beard, concentrate on *becoming aware that you're doing it*. Notice I didn't say try to stop. That comes later, naturally, *after* awareness.

Take Beryl, who called me because she had this "terrible" habit of yanking at her skirt all the time. It happened especially when she was nervous or uncomfortable. It was awkward and tacky, but she just couldn't stop, and most of the time she didn't know she was doing it until some man asked why she was pulling on her skirt like that.

We traced it back to a parental tape.

"Pull down your skirt," her mother would say. Long after the danger of exposing her kneecaps had passed, the habit persisted. Every time she felt uptight around a man, *yank* went the hand to the skirt. Some of her dates felt she was afraid they might try to rape her.

After talking to me, she asked a good friend to help.

"Anytime you see me pulling at my skirt," she asked Linda, "please tell me." Then the two devised a code so that Linda could cue her when they were in public, at a party or a bar or whatever. It was a simple, one-word code. Linda would mention an imaginary friend, "Popsy," and Beryl would know she was tugging at her skirt or had just done it.

She began to connect the skirt-pulling with her emotional feelings. Her nervousness about being around a man who attracted her took shape in that automatic yank on her skirt. Gradually, she taught herself to see it coming, stop her hand, and merely smooth down her skirt. Later on, she eliminated the smoothing motion altogether as she became more comfortable with her feelings and her *self*.

I bet this will surprise you. A lot of people think that they *like* members of the opposite sex when in fact they don't.

Before you continue on with this project of finding love, you should do some self-examination and discover if you truly *like* the opposite sex.

Our society has programmed us to think we like the opposite sex, because it is more or less required if the human race is to continue (and I'm not here discussing the issue of homosexuality, I'm referring to heterosexuals). But, while we are brought up to think that we "ought" to have a partner of the opposite sex, we are *not* brought up to actually *like* them!

Even those who strongly desire their sexual relationships with the opposite sex don't necessarily *like* its members. You'll notice that I'm stressing *like,* not *love.* If you truly like someone, you can forgive a lot, and the liking can get you over the rough spots that are bound to occur in the best of relationships. So how are you going to find out if you like the opposite sex? And what are you going to do about it if you don't?

There are a great many men who don't like women. This is generally more of a problem than women not liking men, perhaps because women are brought up to be dependent on men. And it's much easier to accept being dependent on someone you like than on someone you don't like.

Another thing—and this is the crux of the matter—is that women are brought up to admire and cherish—if not love—men's general characteristics: strength, bravery, manliness, aggression, protectiveness, the competitive instinct and so forth. But men (and women too, alas) are brought up to devalue (or sometimes despise!) women's characteristics: intuition, noncombativeness, passivity, tenderness, and vulnerability. Often men's built-in contempt for women takes the form of seeing them merely as "sex objects" or housekeepers and secretaries. When I told a friend that men tend to want either an ornament or a maid, she said the ideal woman would be an ornamental maid! It's no joke.

Even today, after the so-called sexual revolution and years of women's liberation, there's a whole society out there drumming this into kids' heads. Unfortunately, for most of you, the changes resulting from the sexual revolution haven't yet filtered up to your adult selves.

But new attitudes are afoot, and if you're an enlightened woman, you already know what this leads to. Even some men are beginning to realize how foolish it is to devalue one-half of the population—the half they date, make love with, marry, and have children with. But there's plenty of room for *more* changing, so let's not rest on our laurels! I just want to get the message out there.

But let's stick with this issue of men who don't like women. It's all tied up with one of the first questions I asked you: why are you looking for a mate? If you are *not* looking for a best friend in your mate, you are looking for the wrong reason. True partners are friends. Good friends weather good times and bad, and a firm friendship can get couples over some of the sticky wickets that arise in the bedroom and around the house emotionally.

Why do men grow up not liking women when there are all sorts of reasons why they think they should have a woman? Well, often their reasons for wanting a mate have very little to do with *liking* women. A man may want sexual and domestic services, or feel that a woman will advance his career (hence the term "helpmate"). He may want to show off his power to other men by "getting" a certain type of woman. (The stereotypical image of the cigar-chomping businessman with the fluffy blonde leaps to mind.) A man might want a mother for his children, so he has heirs to pass his name and inheritance on to. He may even want another wage earner to enhance his life-style, on the theory that two incomes are better than one. A female may function as an extension of a male ego—a highly visible one, dangling there from his manly arm. But it is unusual for a man to want a woman because he needs a friend.

There are several reasons for this. While there are many exceptions, it's often true that a man who grew up either as an only child or without sisters of a roughly comparable age is a good bet not to like women much. With all those exclusively male activities filling his childhood, he is much more likely to require that ritual "night out with the boys," and may think of women as functions rather than as people. If the only woman he related intimately to while growing up was his mother, he may tend to think of all women as *mother*.

A man who grew up with sisters near his own age, on the other hand, has suffered some early exposure to the female sex in a natural and nonsexual surrounding. Usually he has learned to like and respect women as human beings not so very different from himself. Since he has had to deal with and fend off sisters he will probably be much more relaxed about his masculinity. If he's had to brush past nylons hanging on the shower bar all his life to get into the shower, he's not going to feel invaded and threatened when he finds a pair of pantyhose hanging from the shower bar of his bachelor pad. (This goes for all female accoutrements—hairdryers, lotions and so on—that send some men into a tailspin.)

Another aspect to this problem of the sexes liking each other is that our society does not encourage boys and girls as children to play together. For boys, playing with girls brings the awful stigma of "sissy." Parents still fear that little boys who play with girls will turn gay, as if by some mysterious process of osmosis. Little boys can be quite friendly and tender to girls as playmates, showing their good masculine qualities of protectiveness and helpfulness quite early, before the ones of tenderness and vulnerability have been stamped out of them. But once parental and peer pressures set in, scorn is brought in to cover up the dangerous tender feelings and actions. *Girls*, they sneer, and up go those defenses that remain in place into adulthood, often for a lifetime. Really *liking* women can be risky business indeed for a male!

Society's tacit deprecation of anything female is also manifested in our training of boys to repress their true feelings. "Don't cry like a girl," the big strong father tells his hurt and snuffly little boy. "Be a man." Who ever says to a little boy, "Charlie, your little friend Mary Jane is kind and loving and gentle and nice, and isn't that wonderful?"

Just like anything else that's locked away and kept secret, being female takes on a slightly evil fascination. If it's so *wrong* to be a girl there must be something dangerously interesting about it. Well, interesting is okay, but it's certainly nothing to *like*. Hidden deep in the dislike is something everybody can relate to. Fear. Fear of what, you may ask? Fear of what women represent.

Men are not entirely to blame for this sad state of affairs. Women, too, contribute to the patterning and programming that teaches children to think that being a girl is really *terrible*. Then when they grow up, we say, "Okay, now go out there and get yourself one of these weak, despicable creatures to make your life and be happy with." Now I ask you, is that logical?

Sometimes when I hold forth on this problem, I meet with incredulous stares, especially from my sophisticated New York friends.

"Sally," they'll say to me, "you must be kidding! This is now. There have been a lot of changes made since the women's movement. Men are more aware now."

Maybe.

Let me tell you a story. I had a call from a young woman in Texas who had called me a few times before. She'd been looking for love, apparently had found it, had married, and was now pregnant. However, she'd not been aware of what I'm telling you here. The man she married was an only child, and he was driving fifty-five miles every day to visit his parents and going out at night with "the boys," leaving her almost totally alone with a difficult pregnancy. On her doctor's orders she quit her job, and so she felt especially isolated.

She asked me what to do. I'm hardly ever at a loss at giving advice, but there just wasn't much I *could* say. Her request that he stay home had only elicited the comment that babies and housekeeping (in this case including yard work) were "women's chores." Short of divorce in the middle of pregnancy, there wasn't much more this woman *could* do.

Clearly her husband doesn't like her very much. Oh, he may love her (in his own way, as the saying goes), but you don't treat a person you genuinely like, your best friend, that way. Do you?

Let's go back to how this all ties in to body language and the way what we express through our bodies nonverbally reflects our deepest feelings and attitudes.

Sometimes men and women don't like each other very much. They may ''love'' each other, in a way that ties loving in with sexual, economical, and social needs, but *liking* in the good old-fashioned way of liking a person as a friend, may be a different matter. Look to how your partner's parents treated each other as a clue. That basic family unit is a powerful shaper of how we tend to view the opposite sex.

If a man's basic attitude is that there is something dreadfully *wrong* with being a woman, it's going to show through his adult façade. There *are* ways you can spot it.

- When he is with his father, are they buddies, ''men together,'' excluding his mother?
- How does he greet his mother? With a dutiful peck on the cheek or a bear hug?
- Is he relaxed and easy with women in general?
- Does his father like women and how does he show it? What are the gestures? Does he hold out the chair for his wife at the dinner table? Take her arm or hand on the street?
- Does his attitude clearly speak of ''women's work'' by avoiding household chores and grocery shopping?
- Does he linger after sex?
- Does he have women friends? Nonsexual relationships that are close?

- When socializing with married couples, does he tend only to talk to the man or does he spend equal or more time with the woman?
- Around children, does he gravitate to the boys or the girls?

These are just some samples. Once you get the hang of it, you'll be able to make up lots of other situations. Even the way a man holds (or chooses not to) a woman's coat says something about his attitude toward women. Today women have given out confused messages—one saying that they don't want to be treated like dolls, another that they want to be pampered. The man who truly likes women will show it in his behavior. He'll touch her a lot in nonsexual ways. Standing or sitting, he'll assume a listening position when she's speaking. Beware the man who's leaning far back in his chair with a faraway look in his eyes when a woman is speaking.

I'd like to take a moment to emphasize that opposite-sex friendships are positive and they're healthy. A lot of people still believe that if a woman and a man are friends, there's naturally a sexual attraction between them or an actual affair, past or present. I'd like to emphasize to my readers, especially the younger ones in college and just starting out in adult life, that it's good to have friendships with people of the opposite sex. You learn a lot, and there's no pressure about sex because there isn't any! This holds true for both sexes—men should have nonsexual women friends and women should have nonsexual men friends. If your sexual partner has such friendships and you're jealous and possessive of the time he or she spends with an opposite-sex friend, look into yourself and examine what insecurities you might be bringing to the relationship.

The points here are equally applicable and important to both sexes. Men and women *together* make up the problem *and* the solution. Being able to spot the person who is not ready to find love will keep you from wasting your time.

Again we return to awareness. What I'm trying to do here is to get you to *think*. And if my young readers believe that this applies only to the "golden oldies" who were raised before the women's movement came along, they are dead wrong. Young men today are as conditioned in this way of perceiving women as they were years ago. Sure, they beginning to be more sensitive, because a lot of young women won't tolerate anything else. But in a great many cases, after the party's over or the night of sensitive lovemaking ends, it's back to men's business. This should change! Corrective action is needed, and this begins in the brain. Remember what I told you about our largest sex organ?

Use it!

If you're a man reading this book, I want you to go out and see for yourself what women are really like. Go *watch* them. See how a woman behaves with her women friends, her men friends, her parents, children, dogs and cats.

I often hear complaints about "nothing to do" from men: "It's so boring watching the old boob tube all the time." Whoa! Let me tell you, fellas, there's a whole species of fascinating animal life out there called *women*.

Research is easy. They're all around you. It doesn't even have to cost you anything. Still, if you get to really *like* her you might want to buy her a cup of coffee. You'd buy your buddy a beer, wouldn't you, without expecting him to go to bed with you?

Try not to think about it in sexual terms. That will be a challenge! Don't ask yourself, "Does she or doesn't she?" (She does, but maybe not with you.) Find out what makes her tick and how it ticks alongside with what makes *you* tick. Ask her advice about something. You might find the experience extremely pleasant and valuable.

Men who have changed tell me that, to their delight, they have discovered that women can be friends as well as lovers. Separately or together. These men have discovered strengths in women and received help from women that they never were going to get from their male buddies. In fact, buddies often aren't true friends. Often they get together in a mutual defense pact. That's why a woman can be seen as a serious threat to buddyhood.

Discovery is exciting. And discovery of women as people can be extremely rewarding.

Now, let's turn to the women out there who don't like men.

Many women have been programmed by their parents (especially the mothers) not to like men. They are taught instead that men are a commodity that a girl has to "get," or worse, "trap" (like a wild animal?) in order to survive. To these women, a man is someone who earns money to support them. In return, they provide sex and housekeeping and mothering services.

They have never been able to see men as friends, are frightened by men's vulnerability (*they're* supposed to be strong and brave, remember?), don't look upon them as equals, and don't consider them friendship material. Their friends are *all* other women.

Then there are the women who have been hurt and disappointed by men, the so-called man-haters, never allowing their wounds to heal, assuming that all men are rotten bastards, out after "one thing." Even the pampered daddy's girls have a distorted view of how men can function in their lives.

Women can be frightened of men and *see* their natural aggressiveness as threatening. Given the number of rapes that occur every day in this country I have to admit that this fear does have *some* basis in fact.

Conversely, there are many women who think that they

are "nothing without a man." The man serves to validate their existence, to give them status in their own eyes. After all, a woman who can "get" a man is a real woman, right?

Many women, following advice given in popluar magazines and books on "how to get a man," think only in those terms. In their minds, even at the very first conversation, they are sizing him up as male/sexual/lover/husband potential. Then they immediately begin trying to figure out *what he wants* them to be, in order to "get" him. And in this twisted process they lose sight of who they are, who *they* want to be.

But this has nothing to do with liking men as people.

Women who have accepted the so-called female role without questioning how it applies to them are stunted in their perceptions of what men can mean to them, how they function both with and without a man. If a man equals only husband-father-breadwinner-protector to a woman, there's no way to get beyond that without changing the mental attitude.

If you're a woman and you get your primary friendship satisfaction only from other women, you've got a problem. Not that women don't make excellent friends. They do. But the same yardstick applies here as when I was talking about men's attitudes earlier. Women need to discover men as friends as well as lovers. They, too, must stop looking at men only as possible lover/mates.

Certainly I realize that it is not possible to separate out sexual attraction in a healthy, normal male-female relationship—*if it occurs*. But be careful—there's no law written that says it *must* occur!

Yet there are women who go off in a huff if every man they meet is not sexually attracted to them. And there are those who feel there's something wrong with them if they are not attracted by the man. "Ye gods!" they shriek, "I'm losing my sex appeal." And down goes the self-image.

You can *see* all of this happening in body language. Watch women. *See* the way they relate to each other, as opposed to how they relate to men. Look out for the subtle gestures. Does a woman touch her woman friends as she touches a man? Is her smile warm and genuine, not always laced with "come-hither"? Does she do little things for a man she's with—maybe hold *his* coat? When she listens, is she really listening or is she just playing the part of the "good listener" because she's been told that's how to get a man?

Watch. And learn.

If you're a woman, ask yourself when was the last time you spent a night out with the boys. Do you have male friends that you rely upon and tell your troubles to, including your love troubles? Without thinking of them in terms of sex?

Incidentally, I want to note here that many sophisticated women have gay men friends. I do myself. Gay men can make wonderful friends for women. Some combine the sensitivity of a female friend with masculine traits. They can be fabulous escorts and are very helpful. Sometimes the tremendous sympathy and understanding they can bring to women comes from having been discriminated against. Gays can serve as a bridge to the male sex for the woman who has a problem confronting straight men as friends.

As long as I'm on this subject, let me also encourage both women and men to also have lesbian friends. A gay woman should not be a sexual threat to a straight woman, and certainly is none to a man. She can be his friend without his feeling he has to "prove" his masculinity by making a sexual overture.

I'm telling you all of this because I'm all for opening up people to each other, and I know that the more freedom you have in your relationships generally, the easier it is to find and relate to that one special person. Although what I'm saying is primarily addressed to the heterosexual, it can be applied to anyone who is looking for love. And everyone has certain fears, biases, and preferences that show up in the way they present themselves to potential mates.

What I'm trying to say is that, in a best of all possible worlds, while recognizing the dangers and understanding the prejudices, I do think one should be open to *friendship*— from any source.

So get out there and keep your eyes open to all those nonverbal visual clues that let you know a lot about another person *before* he/she opens his/her mouth. And speaking of mouths, let's go on to my next topic: *talking*.

4

Go!

NOW YOU'RE ALL SET. You've taken the quiz and found out about yourself. Maybe you've lost a few pounds or bought a new outfit. You've had a great haircut. You've studied your body attitudes and practiced looking and feeling open and accessible instead of closed and unapproachable. You're Ready.

What now?

GO! means getting out there were the action is. And being where the action is means more than going to a party or a bar, to a restaurant or a fancy coffee emporium. It means *talking*.

Conversation is the number one icebreaker. Nobody is going to have a chance to get to know you if you can't open your mouth.

What if you're shy, or just a *wee* bit self-conscious? The prettiest hairdo or the jazziest sports coat isn't going to make up for *that*.

Let's say you're a man who's wise to the fact that women do a lot of grocery shopping. So you go to your local A&P and there you spot a woman you'd really like to meet. If you are the kind of man I think you are, you don't feel you can just go and say, "Can I have your phone number?"

So what do you do? Ask her a question. But make sure it's the kind of question that can lead to more conversation. Don't ask her what aisle the potato chips are in—she might just point and say, "Over there"!

Think. If she's wearing something interesting, ask her where she got it, mentioning that your sister is longing for a sweater just like the one she's wearing. If she says she got it in Italy last summer, you're off and running. Ask about Italy. Tell her you are dying to go. Or you went two years ago. You loved it or you hated it. What did she think? Has she seen the Piazza San Marco or is there a restaurant in the neighborhood that serves really good Northern Italian food? *Anything* to get the conversational ball rolling.

Or suppose you're a woman and you've gone to the health club where there's co-ed weightlifting. You spot this hunk there—or a sweet-looking, not-too-athletic guy who's more your type. (Believe it or not, not every woman *wants* a hunk!) Either way, what do you do?

Go up and smile and say something about the weights. If you're new to the game, ask for advice. (Don't *ever* play dumb.) Say you've just joined up and you aren't sure where to start. Could he make some suggestions? If you're already practically a pro, ask him if he's been in training long. Ask if he runs, or what sort of diet he prefers for exercising. You can always be straightforward. Comment on his muscles. Say you've seen him a few times. Does he live around the neighborhood? Anything to get him talking.

The transition from stranger to friend and perhaps to lover begins with attention—one of you attracts the other, or it's mutual. The next step is recognition—that lingering eye-contact on a crowded bus that sometimes results in ads in the personals column like "You, blonde, 5'2" on MX104 Tuesday P.M. reading *Variety*. Me, 6', glasses, brown hair and eyes. We looked but didn't speak. Call Jeff. 943-8097."

Then comes speaking. Here's another place to pay attention to the other person's signals. By now you should be able to determine pretty quickly by his or her body language whether there's any spark coming from the man or woman you approach, but what about reading the *verbal* exchange— and how can you really start *talking?*

First of all, remember that a first encounter, however dynamic or static, is just that. You have absolutely nothing to lose. If the other person doesn't seem to want to engage in conversation, it doesn't mean you're a nerd or a loser. It might mean he/she has something else on his/her mind, or simply isn't feeling good about him/herself that particular day. Try again, or try someone else. Remember that seeming *desperate* will put an end to even the most promising encounter—fast. Friendly and interested is the key.

You'll quickly feel one way or the other about someone you approach. They'll give off warm or cool signals right away. I remember one day meeting a man on a bus. We were both strap-hanging. He asked me the time and then commented on my Henri Bendel's shopping bag. Did I shop there a lot, and what did I think of the store? He'd seen a blouse he thought his sister might like but he was a bit intimidated. I assured him that the service was pleasant. If I hadn't been involved with someone at the time, I could have offered to accompany him on his shopping trip. As it was, we only chatted pleasantly until my stop, but it made the ride seem shorter.

A woman I know always carries odd, interesting goodies in her handbag. Prettily wrapped sourballs, for example. It's easy to offer someone seated next to you on a bus or plane or train a candy. Few can resist. It's an opener. Or, take my friend Sarah. Sarah suffers from shyness, but she has determined to conquer it. Every day she sees to it that she speaks to at least one stranger. She does not plan these encounters. Sometimes she asks directions, or comments on someone's clothing, or just says *hello*. A friendly hello from a stranger on a busy city street can be a real lift in these impersonal times.

One day Sarah said *hello* to a man at the bus stop, and commented on the two feet of snow they were both standing in. Inspired, Sarah asked him how far he could throw a snowball. A mini-contest ensued as they threw snowballs down the empty street, laughing at the bus's delay. By the time Sarah got off, they'd arranged to meet for lunch the next day.

The moral of Sarah's experience? *Practice*. Go back to that mirror and rehearse little scenes. The scariest things become easier every time you actually do them. They're like muscles, the more you train the better you get. If you were starting an exercize class, you wouldn't expect your unexercized muscles to firm up after just one class, would you? It's the same with learning to speak easily and spontaneously to strangers. Practice—repetition—is the key. The first time you do it, it's going to be difficult, but each successive time it'll get easier, until by the time you've made yourself speak to twenty different strangers under twenty different circumstances, you'll be a pro—it will seem just as natural as walking.

Remember what I said earlier about rehearsing little scenes, in front of a mirror if you like. Or get a friend to play the part of the potential stranger and practice striking up a conversation. Think of yourself as being in a play of your own devising. You're the lead actor, and the director. Actors *rehearse*. Not only do they memorize their lines, they spend hours and hours rehearsing before opening night. And then when the play's running, they still rehearse. They know they can always improve on their performance and they rehearse to keep it always fresh. It's the same with polishing your techniques for feeling easy talking to a likely stranger—on a bus, a train, in a shop, anywhere. Treat it like a muscle—the more you use it, the stronger it will get.

So what do you say once the ball is rolling? *Here's where confidence* comes in. Even if you are a little scared, *fake it.*

By that, I *don't,* most emphatically *don't* mean, *not* be yourself. Just bring a little extra ammunition into the game. You can play a little role. Imagine yourself as a gracious lady or gentleman. Simply *pretend* that you're not afraid to speak to this stranger. And you won't be. A few times out, and the fear itself will be gone. Action is a confidence builder.

Take Jill. Jill is a creature of moods. Ups and downs. Usually she can handle it, but she's in public relations and sometimes she just has to fake a good mood when she's not feeling it.

When she's feeling a little blue and she has to go to a party for a client, she takes extra-special care to be rested and look her best. She summons up a smile by playing with her cat before she leaves. The smile is in place when she walks into the party, and by the end of it all she usually has a good time and finds her bad mood has vanished. It's a matter of *taking control* rather than leaving matters to chance.

Of course, if you're feeling lousy because your boss just told you your pet project has been scrapped (when you were expecting a raise), or your mother has just announced she's moving to Florida and there will be no Christmas at home this year, it may not be exactly the best time to make overtures. Still—if a really appealing guy or girl suddenly looms up on your horizon, someone up there might be telling you that things aren't so bad after all!

Feeling truly rotten is a state of mind—and states of mind can be changed. I warned you in the beginning that we were going to talk about a lot of changes. Well, this is one of them. Not that I expect anyone to be a Pollyanna all the time. I don't. But often a long face and a sad heart are self-indulgences. They hurt only yourself. And they can cut you off from the very experiences that are the cure for what ails you! Which of us hasn't had the experience of brightening up when an interesting stranger popped into our lives?

Let me tell you a story.

Letitia had just moved to New York from a small town in the South. Her love affair of two years had just broken up and she was heartbroken. Fleeing her pain, she decided, finally, to make the break and study acting in the big city. But she wasn't happy.

Not knowing a soul, she arranged to stay in a big hotel while she found her way. One evening, depressed and lonely, feeling defeated, she decided to go down to the hotel's dining room for her dinner, thinking to herself that she was a total failure. Still, she was in New York . . . She sat alone at a small table among the other diners with a book. The hustle and bustle of the dining room made her feel lonelier. She paid the bill and left to return to her room. Sad.

As she stepped off the elevator, a man spoke behind her.

"You didn't have your after-dinner drink," he said.

Letitia turned and stared right into the eyes of a nice-looking man, nicely dressed, smiling politely with mischievous eyes that clearly admired her powder-blue suit and what was in it. She gulped.

"Can I buy it for you?" he asked.

Years of being told not to talk to strangers by her mother and the cold fear of the big city rose up in Letitia. But she was a smart girl—she told her fears to get lost. What could happen in a big hotel with people all around? She smiled.

"I'd love an after-dinner drink."

They spent the evening in the hotel's chic café, talking, dancing and holding hands. He was staying in the hotel, too, and he had a plane to catch early the next day. But he lived across the river in New Jersey. In one fell swoop, Letitia's sadness vanished, life looked brighter, New York seemed friendlier, and success possible. Dan was his name, and when he got back from his trip he called her, and she learned that the Hudson River was no obstacle to love.

What I'm getting at is that if you're shy, you're shy (though there *are* cures) and if you're scared, you're scared. But you can *act* as if you're *not* shy or scared. All you have to do is remember that one time you weren't shy or scared, and replay the feeling. Easy. Well, maybe not the first time, but it gets easier each time.

I had a call one night from a young man who was in despair. Chris complained that he didn't have any dates, couldn't get any. I asked why and he said that he was afraid to ask girls out because he couldn't bear it when they said *no.*

CHRIS: Sally, I just don't know what to do.

SALLY: I think you should try to ask more people out. Ask them out as if they're going to say yes. If you ask them out thinking they're going to say no, they're going to say no. . . . You've got to set a goal: Ask five people out. You think you can do it?

CHRIS: I don't know.

SALLY: Well, wait a minute. . . . Are you ready to accept the challenge?

CHRIS: I'm sort of scared.

SALLY: This is King Arthur and the Round Table and you're Lancelot. Are you willing to accept the challenge?

CHRIS: Yeah, I guess.

SALLY: I guess? Do you think Lancelot would say "I guess" to King Arthur?

CHRIS: Well, he wouldn't say that, but I'm being honest.

SALLY: I don't want honesty. I want bravery. Honesty's not going to get you a date, bravery is. . . . You've got two weeks to ask five girls out, then you call back. . . . Some of the things we have to do in life we do because we have to accept the challenge. . . . What are you going to do to overcome shyness? Don't be shy. Is it as simple as that? Yep.

Life is out there to be enjoyed. Your vocal cords are one of the lovely tools given to you to open doors to other people. Strangers across a crowded room can lock eyes— but if no one makes a move and *says* anything nothing is going to get off the ground.

And while I'm on this subject of talking and asking people out (whether you're a boy asking out a girl or a woman asking out a man), let's hear it for the positive approach! If you're going to ask someone out, ask as if you *believe* they are going to say *yes*. If you expect a "no" answer, and it shows in the way you phrase your invitation, you're likely to get a no. Here are some examples of how *not* to phrase the question.

"I don't suppose you're free on Friday night, are you?"

"You're probably busy on Saturday night, but if you're not, how about going out?"

"You wouldn't want to go for a drink on Tuesday after work, would you?"

These kind of questions pre-program a negative answer. Perhaps a woman or a man doesn't want to admit they aren't busy on Saturday night, or whenever. The half-hearted invitation asks for a similiar response. Also, the other person may think you are only asking them because everyone else already said no! So, make it easy for your prospective date to accept. Give them a wide-open way to say "Yes!"

Say something like, "There's a really great-sounding block party Sunday afternoon. If you enjoy that sort of thing, I'd love you to go with me." Or, "There's a concert in the park Saturday that sounds like fun. Would you like to hear it with me?" Try something unusual— how about "There's a psychic fair this weekend. How about coming along with me and we'll get our cards read?''

Whatever it is, however you phrase it, make it sound 1) inviting to the other person, 2) something you yourself enjoy, 3) like something you could enjoy exploring together.

And while I'm on this subject, let me make a plea for speaking normal English. If you speak your business jargon after hours—whether it's computerese or politicese, stock marketese or medicalese—your chances of communicating with anyone not in your profession is going to be extremely limited. One of the joys of conversation is learning about *others*. Expanding your horizons expands your mind—and opens you up to all those opportunities to find love.

Let's talk about shyness. I've had so many calls about shyness I could write a whole chapter on it. For a country that's known for its aggressiveness in the marketplace, we are a remarkably shy and retiring people!

If you are a wallflower—and believe me there are plenty of shrinking violets among the male population—it's basically because you are down on yourself. You have a bad self-image which translates into low self-esteem. Self-esteem's pretty important. It tells you, not who you *are,* but who you *think* you are. And remember what I said about us being our own worst critics? Low self-esteem is a distorting mirror that, thanks to unrealistic standards promoted by the media, outdated parental judgments and so forth, can transform a minor imperfection into an overall sense of worthlessness.

Often a person enters a party or gathering of some sort and is having a decently good time when the fear strikes.

''If these people find out what I'm really like,'' goes the internal dialogue, ''they won't like me at all.''

This kind of self-defeating, automatic inner tape recording is responsible for feelings of shyness, and subsequently, all sorts of symptoms, from inappropriate giggles to mono-syllabic answers.

Where does this come from? One of the main culprits is the mass-media images that we are all subject to every time we turn on the TV or open a magazine. Too many of us are constantly comparing ourselves to the stars whose famous faces and perfect bodies show up everywhere we look. This media over-saturation produces all kinds of feelings of inferiority in people who have nothing at all wrong with them. They tend to think that if they aren't as clever as the current popular comedian, or as handsome or beautiful as the pop star of the week, then they're some-how inferior. This is nonsense. The world is full of *real people*—and real people are looking for other real people to fall in love with. In addition, many people fear that some social error or *faux pas* will reveal to the world their worthlessness. So they keep their mouths shut tight, or stay home from the party and watch TV. That's safe. No one's going to know if you don't let them in.

That may well be true, but this also means that no one is going to get to know what's *good* about you either. Life is pretty busy for most of us. Prying people out of their shells is time-consuming. Why not pry yourself out of your own shell and save someone else the task? There's no guarantee that anyone else is going to be willing to take on the job anyway, and why should they? You have to do your own work. If you have a sense of personal inadequacy that is stilling your tongue and making you trip over your feet, consider professional help. Put the idea into your think tank right *now*.

Shyness is a form of selfishness. *Ouch! Sally—what did you say? I thought you were a sympathetic person!*

I mean it. There you are, a perfectly nice person with a lot to offer, and you are keeping it from the rest of us by your refusal to talk, open up, let us in. You're indulging yourself in your own misery. If *I* think you're a nice person, might not a lot of other people have a similar opinion? But it's not what I or any others think that is going to make the difference. It's what *you* think of you that matters.

Elaine, a student studying law at a midwestern college, called me one night. She was *terrified* of speaking up in class when her professor called on her. As a result, her grades were suffering and she was panicked about flunking out.

SALLY: Why can't you talk in class? I asked.

ELAINE: Because I'm afraid I'll mess up somehow.

SALLY: How?

ELAINE: Give the wrong answer.

SALLY: But you told me you study hard.

ELAINE: I do. But I still might mess up.

SALLY: Well, what would be so terrible if you did? That's why you're in school, to learn. I don't suppose the professor expects you to know all the answers yet. If you did, you'd be teaching the class, not him.

ELAINE: (She laughed) It's because if I don't know the answer, everyone will think I'm dumb and then they won't like me.

SALLY: Well, all right. Let's suppose they think you're dumb. That's not going to kill you.

ELAINE: Sally, you don't understand.

SALLY: I'm trying. Why would it be so terrible if a few students thought badly of you?

ELAINE: It would mean I wasn't a worthwhile person, that I'd never have a career. I might even flunk.

SALLY: It seems to me you're in more danger of flunking by *not* answering the questions in class. But the world wouldn't end if you flunked either, would it?

ELAINE: My world would end.

SALLY: Why?

ELAINE: Because it would mean I'd failed at something and

then it would prove I'm worthless. There wouldn't be any reason to live.

SALLY: Hold on there. There's always a reason to live. And anyway, you haven't flunked. I've been fired eighteen times in the years I've been in broadcasting. But I always got another job. You're only a failure if you *think* you're a failure.

ELAINE: Yeah, I guess.

SALLY: I know so. You've got to change your thinking all around. Just dump that idea of worthwhile. All humans have worth just by being born. It's the opposite idea you have to get rid of. Worthlessness. Just let it go. When you were a little baby, you didn't have a law degree, but you were still precious and worthwhile—not for what you *might* become, but for what you already were. It's the same now. You just work toward your goals and achieve them. A productive life, doing what you are good at, is all you need.

So, try to forget *yourself* for a minute, especially if you're always watching yourself, and push that shyness away. I'm going to give you some good opening lines and sketch out some hypothetical situations as guidelines. You can take it from there. Remember, *practice* makes perfect!

If you're at a cocktail party and stand next to an attractive person at the hors d'oeuvre table, you might lick your lips and say something like, "My, that pâté's good. What do you suppose is in it?"

He or she just may launch into a dissertation on liver pâté or say that the hostess gets it at a particular gourmet shop. You can then ask about the shop—where it is, what other sorts of food they sell, what's the best time to shop there, and so on.

Another good trick to keep things going is to make a future date to *learn* something from another person.

Let's say you get a conversation going at an antique show and the other person is knowledgeable on the subject. Try telling him/her that you're really interested and would he/she have lunch with you to discuss it (remember, whoever invites *pays*). Keep it cool and in a semi-businesslike tone. You're more likely to get an acceptance if you're not coming on, and lunch is a good way to test the waters in a fairly neutral surrounding. At the very least, you'll learn something to add to your repertoire of conversation topics!

If you live in a big city like New York or Chicago, lunch might be too pricey a way to do your investigating. In suburban areas there are usually plenty of inexpensive restaurants, but if money is an issue, there are alternatives to the same idea, which we'll discuss in greater detail later on. What's important at the checking-out stage is to meet in a public place. That gives you the control over when it starts and when it ends.

Some Surefire Topics of Conversation

- *Animals*. People love to talk about their animals. "Do you like cats (or dogs)?" or even "You look like a cat person (or dog person)." You may find out he/she has a bird. Never mind. They'll talk. Note, too, that part of talking is getting the *other* person to talk. I've got a parrot and I'll talk about parrots at the drop of a feather.
- *Apartments or houses*. People love to talk about how they found their apartment or house, especially in any big city, where apartments are always a hot topic. In the country, it's houses. All you have to do is say, "Do you have an apartment (or house)?" and then ask how they found it. Guaranteed for at least half an hour.
- *Spare-time activities*. Everybody likes to talk about their spare-time activities. Ask advice about your vacation or weekend possibilities. Don't ask what anyone *paid* for a vacation. You can ask if it's terribly expensive, but don't get specific.

- *Shopping* (or where to get anything, especially something unusual). Just ask, "Where did you get that lovely _____?" Be sure to use an appropriate adjective. Or, "Have you any idea where I can buy purple stationery in bulk?" Use your imagination.

Some Topics to Be Avoided

- *Jobs*. Please don't have the first thing that pops out of your mouth be, "What do you do?" I know it's all one hears at parties where strangers meet, but it's judgmental and can be embarrassing. What if the person is looking for a job? Or has just lost one?
- *Love life*. Not right away, please. Don't ask first rattle out of the box if someone's married (or divorced). Look discreetly for a ring if you must, but wait until some conversational water has run under the bridge to broach the topic of someone's love life. He/she might have recently been hurt by a breakup. You don't have to be a therapist.
- *Origins*. "Where are you from?" is another unimaginative question. What difference does it make, in a country where people move a dozen times or more in a lifetime? Trying to categorize a person by birthplace is tacky at best and judgmental at worst. Avoid it.

What this boils down to is this: it's okay to talk about things you or the other person have made decisions about, such as places to vacation or relax, shops, animals, interests. It's *not* okay to ask about things a person had no say in, such as birthplace, or any topics that might be judgmental, such as colleges or jobs.

So get out there and start talking! But first let me help you decide with *whom* to talk.

PART TWO

TECHNIQUES AND TALENTS

5

Setting Priorities

JUDY AND JANET, sisters, took a trip to the shore last summer. They stayed at a beach motel. Every morning, Janet went down to the sand right after breakfast with her sun-tan oil, towel, and her Walkman. She had cassettes of the latest hits. In the early evenings, she spent most of her time relaxing, watching TV, creaming her budding tan, doing her nails, and taking care of neglected beauty routines. Only after ten did she go out looking for entertainment, and sometimes she was too tired for that.

Judy, on the other hand, spent only an hour a day at the beach. She either took a book or just people-watched. In the afternoons, she went exploring. In the early evenings she wandered around the little town talking to people she happened to meet.

Although Janet saw a couple of attractive men at the beach, she later complained that they ignored her. She was one of the shapliest, best-groomed girls on the beach and she knew it. She couldn't understand why no one approached her.

Judy, on the other hand, was invited to a few parties on the spur of the moment by people she talked to in shops or in the local market. She met Ron in a dusty roadside antique shop and now that they're back in the city, they're dating regularly.

Why did Judy, who was actually the less pretty sister, have such a different experience?

The answer is that they had different priorities. Janet was concerned almost exclusively with her cassettes and her beauty routines—in other words, with *herself*.

Getting priorities straight for finding love has to do with realizing that it takes two to tango. The person who is concerned with him/herself to the exclusion of the world around him/her isn't going to find love. Even if it knocks on the door quite loudly, they'll be so involved with painting their fingernails or training their muscles or worrying that they're not measuring up to some hypothetical standard, they won't notice.

Plugged into her Walkman, Janet was in a state of self-created isolation. Bopping in her head to the sound blasting away in her ears, she wouldn't have heard if a man had spoken to her! Preoccupied with attaining bodily perfection *for the future,* she was missing out on romantic opportunities *in the present*.

Judy, on the other hand, had her priorities straight. She was out to find love. Open and ready to meet new friends, she was prepared to go wherever life led her. She hadn't neglected her beauty routines during the winter, so now she could accomplish the daily routine in a minimum of time.

Unrecognized priorities can often dictate your behavior, making it difficult if not impossible for you to find love. In order to connect with another person, we have to be looking for that connection, and to look for connection we can't be self-conscious—we must be aware of *more* than just ourselves.

Self-consciousness takes many forms. A self-conscious

person might make excuses for not going to a party—hair to wash, the bills to catch up on, house repairs, work brought home, anything. I've even known people to *invent* tasks to keep away from social situations!

Janet's own self-consciousness was getting in her way of finding love. While telling herself that she was really just making herself more attractive, she was *avoiding* meeting men. Fearful of not measuring up to some media-syndrome image, she was taking refuge in the *process of preparing for some imagined future love*. Whereas women are probably the worst offenders at this particular game of avoidance, men are guilty too. The classic workaholic is a case in point. Telling himself that he's only working toward the day when he can "afford" to find love, he meantime goes without, finding fault with the women he meets to avoid intimacy; or, if he does fall in love and intimacy threatens, telling the woman, sadly but sincerely, that he is just "too tied up" in his career to have a romance *now*. Thus he defers love to some imagined future.

The point is that life is *now*. Living it on a daily basis is the best way to find love. Self-consciousness masking itself as planning for some idyllic future is a danger—what if that future never comes? Or, what if the right person comes along at the wrong time for your plan? It's another variation on this theme of trying to control the universe. The self-conscious person is standing in his/her own way, and becoming aware of these *unconscious* priorities is the way to adjust them.

Here's a little test that will tell you if your self-consciousness is keeping you from being self-confident.

1. You enter an office where two of your colleagues are chatting. As you walk in, one laughs at a remark you didn't hear and then there is silence. Would you . . .

    a) Ask what was funny?

    b) Think they were laughing about you?

    c) Ignore the situation and stick to business?

2. You are invited to a party by someone you don't know well. Do you . . .

    a) Go expecting to have a good time?

    b) Decide you have nothing to wear and buy an outfit for the occasion?

    c) Give an excuse?

3. You've just met ten new people in a row at a party or function. Do you . . .

    a) Remember all or most of their names and faces?

    b) Have forgotten most of them ten minutes later?

    c) Remember some names/faces but no two together?

4. You find yourself in a stressful situation. Do you . . .

    a) Calm yourself and act competently?

    b) Worry that you're going to fall apart?

    c) Revert to an old habit like nail-biting?

5. You are out on a shopping trip and you spot a man/woman you know slightly and find attractive. Would you . . .

    a) Cross over, say "hi," and start to chat?

    b) Feel that you're really not looking your best?

    c) Try to hide?

6. Your favorite color is:

    a) Whatever I'm in the mood for.

    b) Blue or navy.

    c) Brown or black.

7. The adjective that you'd most like applied to yourself is . . .

    a) Attractive.

    b) Intelligent.

    c) Average.

8. You meet an attractive person of the opposite sex on a train and strike up a casual conversation, during

which he/she says they would like to make love to
you. You feel . . .
a) Amused or flattered.
b) Embarrassed or angry.
c) Frightened or humiliated.

9. Out for dinner in a nice restaurant, you discover you
have been overcharged. Do you . . .
a) Call the waiter and inform him courteously that a
mistake has been made?
b) Pay the check but determine you'll never go *there*
again?
c) Take it as a personal slight and make a fuss?

10. You have inadvertently arrived a few hours early for
a flight. After checking in you . . .
a) Go looking around, find a bar or café where
you're likely to meet fellow travellers and strike
up a conversation.
b) Take your book and go have a cup of coffee.
c) Go straight to the departure lounge and wait.

Scoring

Take five points for A's, three points for B's, and one
point for C's.

40 to 50—A healthy lack of self-consciousness. You are
able to flex to the situation and adjust yourself accordingly
without feeling that *you* are the center of everything.

30 to 40—You teeter on the edge of being self-confident,
but are influenced by what others think of you and fear of
rejection. You need to work on a more positive self-image.

20 to 30—Deep down you are more self-conscious than
you care to admit, and this may be affecting your behavior. Try to remember that others aren't nearly so much
concerned with you as you are. Like you, they are usually
more concerned with themselves. You need to relax more,
be yourself.

Below 20—There's a serious concern here that needs

correcting. You tend to worry too much about what others think and imagine they are denigrating you, so you protect yourself by withdrawing into safety. Come on out—the water's fine. Practice the techniques in this book, especially the ones that help you pinpoint who you really are, and realize that you are in charge of who you are.

Setting priorities is easier than you realize. Once you get the issue of *unconscious* priorities out of the way (such as safety and hiding), then you can go about establishing your *conscious* priorities. And remember what I said at the beginning of this course: You have to make finding love your *first* priority.

So get your head straight. Make a list—as exhaustive as you can—of all the things you want to do and achieve, change or improve, have or acquire. Next, rate those with an A-B-C.

A is Absolute Necessity. *B* is Better With than Without, *C* is Can Manage Without. Rate everything below *C* with a *Q* or a *Z*. *Q* is for Quit Worrying About This One and *Z* is for Zilch—unnecessary.

After you've made your list, put your *A*'s, *B*'s, and *C*'s on separate pages. Then compare the lists and *see* if you want to change your rating of any of them. Perhaps some *A*'s are really *C*'s. The idea is to make a plan based on your priorities. A good plan is one that sets priorities in a workable order and then allows each one to be finished up before the next one moves up. It is not advisable or even possible to work fully on more than one or two *A* priorities at a time.

By the same token, it is easy to work on a dozen or more *Q* or *Z* priorities simultaneously, thereby accomplishing nothing. If you must spend time worrying or feeling guilty, set a timer and then sit there for one hour and do nothing but worry until the bell goes off. When the worry hour is up, go back to working on your *ABC*'s.

Let's suppose your *A* list looks like this:

A-1 Finding love (but I'm not ready)
A-2 Getting a new haircut (I don't know where)
A-3 Losing ten pounds (I'm always trying to lose ten pounds)
A-4 Taking a course in Assertiveness Training (it will help me find love)

The first thing you do is eliminate.

We want to get *A* down to one or two related items, so we assign *B* and *C* to the others.

A-1 Research the best place to get a new haircut.
A-2 Make an appointment to get the haircut.
C   Course in Assertiveness Training.
B   Finding love.

This leaves "losing ten pounds."

If you've been talking about losing ten pounds for ages and have done nothing about it, put that item on the *Q* list and *forget it*.

You get the haircut and, *voila!*, you're learning to set your priorities. The rest is clear. You do whatever else you've decided to do to feel ready, and "finding love" moves up to top priority.

You might be thinking that this is all a lot of work, but if finding love isn't at least as important as your job (you wouldn't go looking for a job without the proper credentials would you?) you're not doing it right.

Finding love requires the same quality and quantity of thought you'd give your career. It's your *life*, isn't it? So—get your priorities in order and then you can *truthfully* say that finding love is Number One.

6

The Unique You

"MAKE AN ENTRANCE," advised actress Tallulah Bankhead. "Even if you have to get caught in a revolving door to do it."

While it's not generally necessary to go that far, each person can develop something special to stand out from the crowd.

Take Bill. He thought he was "just an average guy, nothing special," and because of this he was having a hard time attracting women. When I asked him if he had any special qualities, he answered no. He added that he felt discouraged about finding love because of the competition from better-looking, more aggressive men. And he was shy.

Well, I never give up. After some probing on my part, he admitted he liked to draw caricatures of people he saw.

"But," he hastened to say, "I'm not professional or anything like that. It's just a hobby."

"Fine!"

"I never show my stuff to anyone."

"That's okay. But start taking your sketchbook with

you wherever you go. Keep drawing and see what happens. Can you do that?''

''Sure I can do that.''

''Good. Call me back in a few weeks and let me know what happens.''

Three months later Bill called again. He had been taking my advice, and while at first he had found it a bit difficult, because he was self-conscious, he had talked himself into carrying around his sketchbook until it became second nature. Soon he found his drawing skills improving, and he began to feel more self-confident. Before long he showed a few of his best sketches to a couple of close male friends. They were amazed. Nobody had any idea Bill had this talent. Encouraged, Bill took his sketchbook to a party. He still didn't like to talk much, but soon there was a crowd around him begging for his quick portraits.

One thing led to another. He sketched a young actress while she performed an impromptu skit for the group. No shy bunny she! Later, Bill showed her the drawing and she was enchanted. Turned out that though Marcia could act and dance she couldn't draw a straight line. Her producer was giving a party for the cast of the play she was currently in, and she invited Bill.

There Bill met new people—artists like himself—who he wouldn't ordinarily have come into contact with. He made friends, received invitations. Slowly his shyness receded. It took a few weeks, but he finally asked the ebullient Marcia for a date and she accepted. They found quite a bit in common. Bill drew a whole portfolio of Marcia in different costumes and poses and some of these were used in big blowups hung on the theater's lobby walls.

Bill not only developed a skill, he got a girl, and some commissions! And now he's thinking of quitting his job as a bank teller to become an artist full time, enjoying the company of people like himself.

What Bill discovered, you can too. An artist's drawing

pad is a powerful magnet. Almost everybody is curious to see what's on the paper. You don't have to be an undiscovered Van Gogh to find your unique talent—you only have to be curious, aware, and willing to dig a bit.

A musical instrument is another great attention-getting device. If you play a portable musical instrument, take it along with you. You can always act as if you've just come from somewhere you've been playing it. For example, my friend Jimmy takes his guitar everywhere. Sometimes he just checks it with his coat, but it's always available— and what an asset to a flagging party (or even a lively one) is someone who can make music! Another young man plays the Irish tin whistle, which is a small wind instrument. On it, he can whistle out the merriest tunes, or sad ones about love lost. He—and his wonderful music— are always welcome at any gathering. And there's nothing wrong with this. You aren't being egotistical or trying to draw attention to yourself unnecessarily or hogging center stage. You can give others the gift of your talent—and who doesn't like to be entertained by live music played by a real person right there in the room with you? Sure, we can put on a tape or a record—but the charm of the *personal* is what makes the magic happen. Naturally, if you play the piano you can't take it everywhere you go— but you can take the skill along with you. As anyone who can play the piano even well enough to tinkle out a tune knows, a party that's lucky enough to have a piano player in attendance (and a piano naturally!) is thereby enlivened.

Even if there's no piano, there's a lot of conversation available to the person who plays a musical instrument, and an interest in music can lead to musical history and biography, theory and practice. Opinions are welcome. Anyone, no matter how shy, who's passionately interested in *anything* is usually ready and willing to talk about it.

You say you're not talented? You couldn't possibly learn to draw or play the piccolo? Well, what about taking pictures? Anyone can do that. There are free courses given by some of the big manufacturers (Nikon for one). College photography courses abound. And pictures give everyone pleasure. There are few people who wouldn't respond favorably to someone asking to take their picture (in the appropriate surroundings). And it's easy to ask for someone's name and address and phone number in order to give them a print later.

Then there's my friend Helena. She never goes *anywhere*—not even to the grocery or the cleaners—without a dashing *chapeau*. Her hats are legendary, always causing commentary. She haunts flea markets for ancient specimens of dubious lineage. One day she came home with a gentleman's topper in shiny black silk. Another find was a prewar 1930s feather beret, which she cocks down over one ear. People on the street come up to her and ask where she got her hat.

Or take John. He's got a passion for mushrooms. He has ties printed with mushrooms, a mushroom tie pin, and mushroom cuff links. Almost everywhere John goes, someone asks him about the little insignia, giving him an opportunity to discourse on his favorite topic. At home, his tablecloths and napkins sport mushroom designs. Someone even gave him a mushroom-printed quilt for his bed, beside which stands a mushroom-shaped lamp.

If a hostess wants a recipe, she has only to call John for the last word on mushroom soup or barley-mushroom burgers. John has taken many a date a-hunting the wild species, an art unto itself. He even set himself up in a tidy little sideline business selling the wild varieties—which are not available commercially. These interests have put him in touch with a wide variety of people that his work as a computer programmer wouldn't have.

He talks to pickers in Minnesota and sells wild mushrooms to top chefs in New York, who have become his friends because he's offering a unique service.

When John decided to write a book about his favorite fungus friends, he had no trouble finding a publisher. The editor suggested a woman artist for the illustrations and in the course of his teaching her about mushrooms, love bloomed. Now they're housekeeping together, and John has a constant audience for his culinary expertise. Mushroom paintings adorn their apartment. It's a perfect match.

You see? All you need is to take a good look at yourself and find out what's there to work with. Some of those little quirks of yours—you might have thought of them as harmless but useless—might serve the purpose. No one has to be restricted to endless hours of TV or "escape" reading. There's plenty inside each of us to develop and use—it's only a matter of ferreting it out and learning to work on what you already have.

So how do you go about finding an interest? For starters, ask three people to tell you what they consider unusual or interesting about yourself. You don't need artistic talent to stand out: you need to consider and capitalize on your assets. Take my best friend Bart. He's a trivia maven. If it's a lot smaller than a breadbox and something you'd never find around the average house, Bart knows about it (or at least where to go to find out about it).

Bart's ruling mania to know everything there is to know about nothing worth knowing led him into a conversation with the publisher at the local newspaper, and now he writes a weekly column called "The Fleabag," in which he expounds about the little-known details of whatever's happening in town that week. This has produced a slew of telephone calls and invitations—"could you find out this or that?"—from individuals and organizations, thus expanding Bart's range of social contacts.

Remember, the best cure for the shy person is to become an expert at *something*. Expertise gives confidence; confidence leads to outgoingness; outgoingness creates new friends; friends increase self-esteem . . . and self-esteem is the magical attracting power.

7

The Importance of Clothing

IS THERE A person alive who hasn't at one time or other
(maybe every day) moaned, "What *shall* I wear?"

There are hordes of people out there with bulging closets
. . . who still insist that they *never* have *anything* to wear.

Clothing plays many roles in our lives. It is a language
all its own, serving some of the same nonverbal purposes
as our "body language."

First, clothing announces sex, age, and class to even the
most casual observer. But it is also a powerful indicator of
such things as occupation (think of the pinstripe-suited
banker or the carpenter with his array of tools hanging
from his pants), origin, personality (that guy in the red
blazer is quite a dashing fellow), opinions, tastes (the
woman in the severe navy blue suit with matching handbag
and shoes is making a no-nonsense statement about herself), sexual desires (no explanation needed here!), and
current mood.

But clothes go beyond merely identifying us. They serve
to define and describe us.

*We must package ourselves in order to get what we
want.*

93

Personally, I'd rather this weren't the case. I'd like us all to be recognized for our sterling qualities without bothering about the package they come in. But it just ain't so. Just as you wouldn't give someone a diamond ring wrapped in a plain brown paper, you wouldn't wear baggy old jeans to a black tie dinner party.

Clothes may not the man or woman make, but they do reveal a lot about your personality and what you think of yourself, even if at the moment your attire is saying "I don't give a hoot how I look today," or "I'm too bloody tired to bother." They can also be a very effective tool to make a statement or deliver a message.

When a man comes home from the office to find his wife/girl friend wearing a see-through peignoir, he knows she isn't planning a quick trip to the supermarket before dinner. And when a man arrives for a date wearing a fresh, long-sleeved white shirt, he doesn't have to be carrying roses to indicate to his lady friend that, at least from his point of view, the evening is going to be special.

Remember what happened the first time you crawled out of your jeans and into a prom dress or a tuxedo? *Transformation*, that's what. You became someone you didn't know you were—or had only dreamed of being.

Sometimes these transformations are unwelcome or serve to mask rather than reveal the true self. Think of all those past generations of children squirming in their "Sunday-go-to-meeting" finery, hating every moment. Many's a corporate executive playing the "man in the grey flannel suit" on the job and secretly longing for his own private, perhaps even rather eccentric after-work garb.

Then there's the type who *never* takes off his/her occupational suit—doctors and lawyers, for example. Young doctors from the hospital in my neighborhood can be seen on the street at every hour of the day and night in their hospital suits, stethoscopes dangling from their pockets or necks.

Proud they are of their life's work—and their clothes announce this to the world. An engineer friend of mine *always* carries a mini-slide rule in his pocket—no matter what the occasion.

The doctor's white coat and the slide rule are *conscious* statements—but, alas, there are many *unconscious* things we say about ourselves through our mode of dress. And sometimes if we want to say a different thing about ourselves, we need to change what we wear and how we wear it.

Let me tell you about Dan.

A successful metropolitan executive, tall and lean, he is in really good physical shape, kind and generous and a delightful companion. Why, then, was he having so much trouble finding love?

In a word: *packaging*. Though his inner qualities were known and appreciated by his close friends, he was projecting an image of quite a different person. Brought up in a home where clothing was considered to be an affectation if it went beyond the bounds of simple comfort and durability, Dan was—to be honest—shabby-looking.

I'd seen this man spend a hundred dollars on luncheon for two without even a glance at the check. He vacationed in exotic places like Hong Kong and Peru, and bought expensive presents en route. Yet, to look at him, you'd have thought he barely managed to make ends meet! The last time he bought a suit must have been five years ago, and that one was off the rack. Inside him there was real gold, but that plain brown wrapper was hiding it. There just weren't any females interested in unwrapping his unattractive package to find out what was inside.

Does this sound familiar? If so, you might need some repackaging yourself!

Think of items you purchase regularly—food and cosmetics, liquor and wine, magazines and books. These industries spend millions of dollars on packaging—for one reason only: to get you to buy what's in the package. Now, if you had to choose between two boxes of chocolates that were exactly alike except that one was a bright red and gold box with a girl dancing on it, and the other was plain gray cardboard, which would you pick?

Well, it's the same with people. We are beguiled, intrigued, entranced, and attracted by the plumage they display. Most of us will turn to look at an especially attractively turned-out person on the street or in a store or restaurant. Yet, when it comes to ourselves, we bungle along in a state of confusion and anxiety, even if we have closets bulging with clothes (or maybe *because* we have bulging closets!). What looked good in the shop looks terrible when tried on at home. Nothing goes with anything else. We buy new outfits constantly, none ever quite solving the problem. In some cases, economic ruin threatens. This is especially true of young persons fresh out of school who are still searching for their true identity.

Paula, working on a graduate degree at a major university, was still wearing her clothes from high school and looking very much like a young, inexperienced girl, even though she was in her thirties and worked as an editor for her university department. Why? Paula still identified herself as a *student*, though she was herself an instructor. Her little-girl clothes told the world that she didn't yet consider herself an adult.

Her excuse was that the ones she had "would do," and that spending money on new ones wasn't necessary, even though she could afford them. When her aunt made her a gift of some beautiful and fashionable silk dresses she refused to wear them. Silk was too extravagant, it wasn't practical, she had nowhere to go that required dressing up.

Behind Paula's apparent sensible attitude was a deep fear of having to function as a grown-up. As long as she was just a student, she was not required to take full responsibility for herself. As a graduate student, even though she was self-supporting, she was still nominally under the protection of the university, an extension of parental authority. Her clothes reflected this—and she wondered why her students didn't take her seriously! Men, too, were given the indirect message that Paula was not a mature woman. Paula couldn't understand why she attracted immature men who weren't ready for commitment. Can you?

Dress isn't just a matter of wearing the appropriate gear for the occasion. The way you dress exposes (or conceals) different aspects of yourself. Choosing your wardrobe offers you a unique opportunity to explore your personality and mood.

Take Julia—a legal secretary who is required by her job to dress conservatively. She's very feminine, longs for ruffles and frills. By day, with the regulation suit, she settles for small touches to express her personality. Blouses of pure silk, a pretty handkerchief for her purse, light perfume. Evenings and weekends she allows herself to indulge in long caftans beruffled and flowing for loungewear, and for evenings out, soft, frilly blouses and full skirts in rich materials. This way she can have the satisfaction of expressing aspects of herself not permitted in her nine-to-five life.

Most men are quite happy to get out of their standard, everyday suits and climb into whatever leisure-wear they find comfortable, but George is another matter. A dandy at heart, George works as an auto mechanic, a job he loves and does well. Daily he climbs into his overalls, and nightly removes the grease-stained garment for the pleasure of dressing in a suit and a clean white shirt, even if he's only going to the movies with a buddy or hanging out at his local pub. It makes him feel good and he can enjoy his overalls the next day, knowing that they represent only his occupation, not him.

Put some thoughts into what expresses you. And think about the sort of person you'd like to attract. If you truly appreciate a quiet, sober individual, flashy and seductive clothes could put that kind of person totally *off*. On the other hand, you can dress in a way to show you are an interesting, exciting person.

A word of caution. If at heart you are a quiet type who wants to get to know someone before beginning a sexual relationship, don't dress like a casual lay. If you're whimsical, don't dress conservatively because you think that will attract the "right" sort of person. He/she will be wrong for you.

Be honest—but give yourself the benefit of the best that you can be. Think, for example, of the man who always wears black rubbers over his shoes, even when it's not raining (it *might* rain, right?). Automatically, he would be classified as fussy and a bit dull.

But imagine him in some classy, well-polished leather loafers. *Voila!* with one small alteration he instantly becomes more attractive and accessible.

SALLY'S BASIC RULE

Keep it simple. Stick to natural fabrics whenever possible. (Some synthetics are excellent for travel and practicality, but avoid polyester.) Classic cuts and fabrics such as wool, silk, cotton, linen are best. Don't attempt to be always in the latest fashion. It's expensive, changes often, and the look may not be for you. Find what suits you and stay with it. Make sure that what you have coordinates.

Here are a few *dos* and *don'ts* for dressing (and undressing!) for both sexes.

WOMEN

Don't wear tight jeans if you think you're going to end up in bed with him. There's not a man alive who has figured out how to get a woman out of those skintight coverings, no matter who's on your designer label. The same goes for pants in general, unless they are soft of fabric, easy of cut, and elastic of waist.

Don't wear a front-hooking bra. The poor guys have already spent years perfecting their technique for popping you out of your old-fangled back-hooking one. Being expected to develop an instant new technique isn't fair—and it's enough to cool a man's ardor.

Don't dress in anything impossibly fragile and/or complicated. Remember, too, that certain clothing just screams, "Don't touch."

Do be aware that this might be the night your relationship progresses to a first sexual encounter. Spontaneity is fine, but a little planning is in order to make things go smoothly. This is not the time for feelings of awkwardness or unnecessary fumbling.

Do be fresh from the skin out. Undies are important, whatever style you choose. Rips and stains and soils are *out*. There's a whole literature on the importance of female underwear, and it's beyond the scope of this book, but you need not go for the fancy, sexy kind unless this is how you really are. Simple white cotton with a touch of trim is coming back, and the word's out that the men are finding it a terrific turn-on!

Do pay attention to details. Hems and zippers, buttons and hooks, should all be in good condition and working order. The zipper that sticks, the button that won't unbutton, can dampen the most romantic atmosphere. And "Here, let *me* do it!" does *not* exactly grease the wheels of romance.

MEN

Don't, whatever you do, fail to be fresh and clean. Fancy colognes are optional—a man smells good just as he is out of the shower. Clothing, too, should always be well-pressed and the shirt *must* be clean.

Don't wear white boxer shorts that are too long. They are funny looking to women who do not find them sexy. Opt for bikinis unless you have a paunch to hide, in which case find a middle ground.

Don't walk around in your socks and underwear. Take the socks off *first*. There's as much art to a man's undressing as there is to a woman's.

Do wear a clean, white, long-sleeved shirt—especially on the first date. This signifies at once that you care, find the occasion important, and are respectful.

Do carry a clean, white handkerchief. Women may use tissues but a handkerchief still says something about a man. Cotton will do, but linen is best with or without monogram or trim.

Do wear proper footgear. Running shoes are for running and are glaringly out of place with most clothing. Women look at men's shoes and judge them accordingly. Dirty shoes (especially your well-worn sneakers or running shoes) say "dirty feet" to a woman. I can't tell you how many phone calls I've taken over the radio from women complaining about this one item of clothing. Even if a man went home, showered, shaved, and put on clean jeans and a clean shirt, if he then put on his old dirty (and by extension smelly) sneaks, he looks less than clean to a woman. This message is especially for young men under 30, although it applies to everyone. *Don't,* repeat *don't* wear your running shoes/sneakers on dates. It's a definite turn-off.

PART THREE

CONSIDER YOURSELF

8

What's Your Style?

YOU'D BE SURPRISED how many phone calls I get about matters of "lifestyle." She's an executive and he's a plumber—will it work? (Give it a try, I say.) Or he's an avid tennis player and her idea of strenuous activity is watering the houseplants. Will the relationship thrive? (He can play tennis with a buddy.)

Not since *My Fair Lady,* when Professor Higgins set out to prove that the only difference between a flower-seller off the street corner and a high-born lady was proper pronunciation of the English language, have matters of style seemed so important to so many people.

But how important is "lifestyle," and what does it have to do with finding love?

Style is an amalgam of many things, some of them of lasting value (and therefore of utmost importance) and some that are temporary, to be shed along the path to maturity.

The younger you are, the more important superficial matters of style may seem—such as dressing in the current fashion, going to the "in" places, seeing the latest movie, or buying the newest record.

The style that has to do with deeper values reflects our backgrounds and what naturally attracts us. *True* style is personal. As we get older, we learn that dressing has little to do with fashion and everything to do with who a person is. Tastes will always differ widely, but one's preferences are a reflection of inner values. ''In'' places may change, but the person, the self, remains.

Your style—what you present and how—will affect who you attract and to whom you're attracted. Knowing your own style comes first. Finding out if your style is a true representation of your *self* is next. Style can give out strong hints about what you value and want—or it can be used to cover up, conceal, hide. If your style does not show others who you really are, it might be affecting your ability to find love.

Here's a checklist to help you draw in some more strokes in your own ''personal profile.'' There are no right or wrong answers. Just be *honest*. You're trying to take a good look at yourself to see what you're projecting, what's the true you, and what can be changed. Mark the statements with a *T* for True, an *F* for False, or an *O* for Doesn't Apply.

APPEARANCE

I'm uncomfortable unless I'm stylishly dressed in the latest fashion. _____

I'm a casual type. Dressing up doesn't interest me very much. _____

I consider myself above-average in attractiveness. _____

Neatness and cleanliness go a long way with me. _____

I admire fitness. I'm in shape and plan to stay that way. _____

Specific physical qualities (height, weight, hair/eye color) always attract me. _____

I'm always attracted to the same type. _____

Character means more than appearance. _____

I'm generally pleased with my appearance. _____

A good personality is more important than looks or fancy clothes. _____

I judge people by their clothes. _____

PERSONALITY

I like to laugh and have a good sense of humor.   _____

I like conversation and am very verbal.   _____

I'm more of a spectator than a participant in conversations.   _____

Thoughtfulness is important to me. I remember anniversaries and birthdays.   _____

If I want something, I just ask for it.   _____

I'm an outdoor type and need to share outdoor activities with my partner.   _____

Socializing is an important part of my life. I go out a lot.   _____

I need time to be alone frequently.   _____

I'm a definite night person.   _____

Introspection is a regular practice.   _____

Being with strangers is easy for me.   _____

I like to flirt.   _____

It takes me a while to get to know someone.   _____

I'm usually cheerful and optimistic.   _____

I'm an introvert.   _____

I like crowds and group activities.   _____

I'm a beach person.   _____

Camping and hiking vacations are best.   _____

I love my garden.   _____

Candlelit dinners appeal to me.   _____

I like to be in the midst of a lot of activity.   _____

I'm an early riser and like sunshine.   _____

Long, solitary walks give me time to think and
reflect.   _____

I wish more people were like me.   _____

There's never enough time in the day.   _____

I'm often fatigued or overtired.   _____

I prefer mental activities to physical.   _____

I consider myself to be flexible to others' needs.   _____

SEX

Sex is important to me and I like it as frequently as possible.   _____

I like sex with an older person best.   _____

I am inexperienced in sex and need someone to teach me.   _____

I like sex but there are more important things in life.   _____

My idea of perfect sex is on an exclusive basis.   _____

I can easily discuss intimate matters.   _____

My emotions are very close to the surface.   _____

I like to talk about sex.   _____

I have definite sexual preferences and don't hesitate to speak about them.   _____

Certain sexual practices just don't appeal to me but I'm hesitant to say so.   _____

I like to initiate sex.   _____

The idea of getting too close to someone puts me off.   _____

My partner's age affects how I feel sexually.   _____

I like variety in sexual partners.   _____

Our sex life is secondary to the other aspects of a relationship.   _____

I am very open to discussing my sexual needs with my partner.   _____

I am constantly open to learning about what turns my partner on.   _____

I consider sex to be a topic that nice people don't discuss.   _____

My parents had a good sexual relationship.   _____

My sex relationships have generally been good.   _____

One or more of my previous partners have complained that I'm not sexy enough.   _____

I'm often complimented on my sexiness.   _____

Most people put entirely too much emphasis on sex.   _____

I'm offended by sexual invitations before I really know a person.   _____

Pornography turns me on.   _____

EMOTIONAL MAKEUP

I have my emotions under control most of the time.   _____

It's essential for me to talk freely about my feelings.   _____

I'm emotionally open with others.   _____

Emotional involvement and sex are not the same thing.   _____

I like to reach out to others and help.   _____

People often ask me for favors.   _____

I hate constantly analyzing my feelings.   _____

I'm considered a good listener.   _____

I'd like to become more communicative.   _____

Sharing emotions is very important to me.   _____

I am affectionate and show a lot of love.   _____

I like to give presents to those I love.   _____

I expect to receive presents from a lover.   _____

I need affectionate gestures from a lover.   _____

I come from an affectionate family.   _____

I always hug my friends.   _____

INTELLECTUAL/EDUCATION

I consider myself of above-average intelligence.   _____

I am an intellectual, not a dreamer.   _____

I believe in being practical.   _____

I have a college education.   _____

My friends are all as smart as I am.   _____

I think education is a lifelong process.   _____

Learning new things is important to me.   _____

I like to talk about controversial subjects, like religion and politics.   _____

I would rather listen and learn than show off what I know.   _____

I'm eager to talk about my interests.   _____

I'm not much of a thinker but I've a lot of creative imagination.   _____

I have an artistic temperament.   _____

I would like to get more education.   _____

People who are smarter than I am intimidate me.   _____

HABITS/SOCIAL LIFE

I'm a nonsmoker and hate to be around smokers.   _____

I smoke but can abstain if others object.   _____

Smoking is important to me and nonsmokers who object give me a pain.   _____

I don't drink alcohol and don't want to be with anyone who does.   _____

I drink moderately but don't push drinking.   _____

Drinking is an important part of my social life and I don't want a nondrinker.   _____

(If you use drugs, which I hope you don't, the same questions apply.)

Socializing is an important part of my life. I like to go out at least four nights a week.   _____

Time alone is important to me.   _____

Proper manners in public are important.   _____

I expect people to call if they are going to be late for an appointment or date.   _____

I'd basically rather talk than listen.   _____

I like to be the center of attention.   _____

I have some quirky but harmless personal habits, like sleeping with a special pillow.   _____

I am absolutely inflexible about my (any) routine.   _____

Previous partners have complained about my personal habits.   _____

Other people's habits get on my nerves.   _____

I'm not a creature of habit. I'm flexible.   _____

My clothes are usually kept in order.   _____

My desk is always messy.   _____

I like to keep my own things separate from others'.   _____

I'm tolerant of other people's idiosyncrasies.   _____

I'm neat, but messy people don't bother me.   _____

I'm a compulsive cleaner-upper.   _____

My mother was a good housekeeper.   _____

My parents loved to give parties.   _____

My favorite home entertainment is the TV.   _____

HOME/ENTERTAINMENT

I love animals to be part of my household.   _____

I like to spend most of my home time with someone special.   _____

My home reflects my personality accurately.   _____

I love to entertain at home.   _____

I don't know how to/don't like to cook.   _____

Eating in restaurants is a favorite hobby.   _____

My main goal is a beautiful home.   _____

Home is where I hang my hat.   _____

My idea of the perfect vacation is some exotic
spot far away from home.   _____

I like to spend a lot of time at home alone.   _____

My friends like to visit my home.   _____

I frequently visit my friends' homes.   _____

Home decorating interests me very much.   _____

Camping out—indoors or out—suits me.   _____

I'd move in with someone I fell in love with.   _____

WORK/FINANCES

I'm only interested in someone whose job status is as high or higher than my own. _____

My occupation is a considerable source of pride and satisfaction. _____

Earning a lot of money is important because that's the only way you can be secure. _____

I'm a workaholic. _____

I work because I have to earn a living. _____

My work doesn't pay much but I love it. _____

My partner's work is of equal importance to me as my own. _____

I'd really like to start my own business. _____

A good job is one of the most important things in life. _____

I travel a lot in my work. _____

Business travel is very enjoyable to me. _____

I like sharing my work experiences. _____

A love relationship would always take precedence over work with me. _____

FAMILY/FRIENDS

My parents want me to visit regularly and this contact is important to me. _____

I spend quality time with my children. _____

I have raised a family and now want to spend my time with a love partner. _____

I want to have children. _____

I love children, whether my own or someone else's. _____

I spend every major holiday with my family. _____

My family is not very close to one another. _____

I've always had good relationships with the families of my lovers/husbands/wives. _____

I think it's more important for couples to be with each other than with families. _____

Family just isn't an issue with me. _____

My friends are very important to me and I like to spend a lot of time with them. _____

Even when in a love relationship, I like a night out with the boys/girls. _____

It's okay for lovers to have different friends. _____

My friends have generally liked my lovers. _____

I don't have close friends.   _____

My friends are all of long standing.   _____

My lovers have generally liked my friends.   _____

I never introduce a lover to my friends.   _____

It's important that my friends approve of my lover.   _____

I can have love relationships separate from my friendships.   _____

I want my lover to be my best friend.   _____

INTERESTS/HOBBIES

I enjoy solo sports like horseback riding or swimming. _____

I enjoy hours of quiet reading. _____

I spend a lot of time on the phone with business associates or friends. _____

Watching sports on TV is one of my favorite pastimes. _____

I am a music lover and go to concerts frequently. _____

I don't have many interests outside my work. _____

My hobbies take up all my free time. _____

I like to keep up with world events, reading a newspaper and watching the news daily. _____

I'm always taking a course in something. _____

I play a musical instrument. _____

I like doing things by myself. _____

I love to exercise. _____

Now that you've completed the checklist, go back over it and reconsider your answers. Are there any you want to change?

Next, construct a portrait of yourself as it emerges from the answers. Pretend that you are writing an advertisement for the personal column and that you are going to describe yourself to a total stranger whom you hope to attract. Have in mind what this person might be like. (This isn't going to be easy! Even the simplest person is amazingly complex.) As you draw your self-portrait in words, jot down anything else you think about yourself and your lifestyle that isn't covered by the checklist. See what you like and what you don't like, what you might want to change. Think about the kind of person who would be attracted to the person you have described (yourself).

Must you find someone with the exact same lifestyle as your own? The answer to this question will affect not only whom you look for, but where you go to look. If you have a very active, sports-oriented lifestyle, you wouldn't go to a museum lecture or a classical concert of fifteenth-century wind instruments to look for a like-minded partner. But how like-minded must a partner be? If you are a very family-focused person, involvement with a loner could be disaster. On the other hand, it could spur you to become more independent.

The trick is to go for balance. Two people who are *exactly* alike will eventually bore each other if each becomes too predictable. On the other hand, partners with completely different lifestyles (and value systems) may spend all their time arguing. The best mix is when the partners can open each other up to new experiences. As I've said, it stands to reason that if you aren't open to encountering new experiences, you'll narrow your own field of opportunity.

Take a closer look at your self-portrait. Does it represent the "real" you? For example, if you're a fashion plate, is it because you love clothes or because you're afraid to be out of step with the crowd?

Now go over the checklist one more time and make a list of all those things you couldn't/wouldn't change—not for the most perfect Mr./Ms. Right. This is the *core* you. Then mark the characteristics you'd be willing to modify.

That's your flexibility factor. Lastly, mark those you'd be willing to change. (If you're a slob, would a little neatness kill you? If you're an ashtray polisher, couldn't a little disorder loosen you up a bit?)

The trick, again, is *awareness*. That's the way to find—and maybe change—your style. Now for some other things you need to know to find love . . .

9

Does Character Count?

YOU BET it does!

Who you are definitely affects whom you are going to attract. It's not really true about opposites attracting, not in terms of character. Like attracts like. Nice people want other nice people.

We all wear masks occasionally. It couldn't be otherwise in society, where negative feelings must sometimes be contained in order to grease the wheels of progress and industry. Good manners help us through life. We may have to pretend that Great-Aunt Lilly's atrocious Christmas present is just what we've been wanting all along, but we don't have to live with Aunt Lilly.

But an intimate situation is quite another story, and *you can't change the rules once you're into it*. So the only way to go is to start out honestly. *Without masks*.

You've just analyzed your personal style—and if you've been honest with yourself so far you're beginning to get an idea of who you are and what you want out of love.

Who are you? Are you trying to be someone you're not because you think it will increase your chances of finding and keeping love?

Too many people think that, if they pretend, it will help them to find a mate. This is a course doomed to failure. If you're pretending to be someone you're not, you are going to attract (and possibly *get*) the wrong person.

True, some people consistently misrepresent themselves, and we've all been fooled at one time or another, but the clearer you are about yourself and the clearer you can be about another person, the more likely you are to spot falseness and avoid it. But if you're preoccupied with keeping your own mask in place, you may not notice the other person doing the same thing—until it's too late.

There's another type of fantasy-person. This one pretends *to him/herself* that he/she is sincere. It's pretty easy to get caught in another person's *unconscious* fantasy. It's not that the person is lying to you—he/she is lying to him- or herself because it's what he/she truly wants to believe. Convincing themselves, they then convince you. This happened *to* a friend of mine. She was with a perfectly nice man, or so it seemed. He was dynamic and exciting, flew around the world on his job, and blew into town periodically armed with flowers, wine, and charm. Two weeks into the romance, he asked her to marry him. Prudently, she wanted to wait a bit. She decided in his favor, but when she told him she was ready, the excuses began. Throughout, he assured her he *wanted* to marry her, just as soon as possible, and, I've no doubt, believed it himself. It took her too long to *see* that she'd become caught in his fantasy. It was three years before she came to realize that they were *never* going to set the date; what he liked, as a balance to his perpetual-motion lifestyle, was the *idea* of marriage, not the reality. I'm sure he didn't consciously set out to deceive her any more than she helped, by accepting his excuses year after year, to deceive herself. And waste a lot of time. Partly it was out of her own need for the excitement of a roller-coaster affair, but she wasn't paying attention to her need for commitment and stability in a relationship as well. If she had been, she'd have pulled the plug on his act a lot sooner.

The lesson here is that the clearer you are about yourself, the clearer you can be about another person, the more likely you are to spot falseness—intended or benign—and avoid it.

Remember the unconscious signals we give off with our body language. Even if you are trying to cover up and pretend, you are going to be letting people know the truth about you in other ways. And even if you succeed in a masquerade, you'll be too busy working on your false image to have a good time or recognize the right person. And if you are being the best person you can be, you stand a far better chance of attracting someone else who is being the best person he/she can be. If you are going to be dishonest about yourself, you are going to be in deep trouble.

Let me give you an example of what *not* to do.

LOUISE: Hi, Sally. I've got a real bad problem. Can you help me?

SALLY: Okay. Tell me about it.

LOUISE: Well, it's kinda hard to talk about.

SALLY: Why?

LOUISE: Because I'm ashamed of myself.

SALLY: What have you done?

LOUISE: Well, for the past year and a half I've been living a lie. Pretending to be what I'm not.

SALLY: Why did you do that?

LOUISE: I was trying to impress my boyfriend.

SALLY: Did he believe the stories you told?

LOUISE: I didn't really tell stories . . . I just did a lot of things that weren't me.

SALLY: Like what?

LOUISE: Oh, I pretended everything was great even when it wasn't. And I never said anything, even when he hurt

me. I ran around buying him gifts and telling him he
was wonderful all the time. I guess I just about babied
him to death.

SALLY: So what's the problem now? Didn't he like that
kind of treatment?

LOUISE: Oh, he likes it okay but now I want to be the real
me before it's too late. And I'm afraid if I am, he'll
walk away.

SALLY: Then you don't want to keep on flattering him?

LOUISE: No. I want him to know I love the real him. I
don't mind his faults. I just don't want to keep pretending he hasn't got any.

SALLY: Then you've got to tell the truth. Kindly. You have
to first be honest with yourself, and then you have to
level with him. You don't have to make a big confes-
sion, just slowly begin being yourself until you get
comfortable with it. Chances are he won't even notice,
or if he does he'll be glad. Don't forget—you're putting
a big strain on him, too, by pretending he's Superman.
He has to live up to that and if you don't think you're
good enough just being you, he may be having the same
problem. So you're both caught in the pretending trap.

LOUISE: Thanks, Sally. You really made me feel better.

SALLY: Are you going to do it?

LOUISE: Well, it's pretty scary. But I want to try.

SALLY: Let me tell you what to do. I call it taking a beat.
When you find yourself not being honest, and you know
what's going on in your head, stop yourself for a moment. Ask yourself the question, Why am I doing this?
That beat—the moment—is often enough to stop yourself and start over. Try it. It works.

LOUISE: I will.

SALLY: Good girl!

It's important to realize that in the intimacy of a relationship it's hard to hide the facts over a long period of

time. Think of the strain you put yourself under trying to keep your mask on straight!

In the final analysis, you have to be *happy* with whomever you choose as a mate or lover. And when the "dating game" is over, if you've deliberately created a wrong image, you'll be stuck with it.

So be yourself. Don't lie. Don't pretend to your partner that you're just crazy about Sunday afternoon football if you're really longing for a classical music concert. Don't pretend you just love shopping for ladies' lingerie when the very thought sends you into a catatonic state.

If you don't accept who you are, you aren't going to make any changes, and genuine change is the only route to self-improvement. No amount of pretending can alter you, but you can make any number of changes you want after you recognize the need to change.

I want to talk a bit about why people wear masks. It's called the "If these people knew me as I really am, would they like me?" syndrome. Fortunately, there's a cure for this ailment, and it's called *Know Thyself.* After *that* comes *Improve Thyself, Be Thyelf,* and *Trust Thyself.*

What do you think is the sexiest, most attractive, most appealing quality in a person of the opposite sex? Good looks? A warm smile? Sharp clothes? A trim, fit body? Perfect features perfectly made up or groomed? A charming personality? Or is it that *indefinable* something?

If you picked the last item on my little list, you are right. That indefinable quality means you know who you are, you've improved who you are, you like who you are, and you trust who you are. You don't have to pretend to be anything or anyone else.

If you've got it, everybody knows you've got it. You know what it looks like—*feels* like—when a person walks into a room and everybody turns to look, not because of anything special about that person's appearance, but because of something special about how he/she *is*. Another word for it is *presence*.

What if, when you drew up your self-portrait in Chapter Five your reaction was *Ugh!?* The following test should help you.

Check Your Self-esteem

1. You are promoted to boss after having worked in the ranks. Your response is
   a) "Oh goody, I made it. Now I can run the show."
   b) "Gee, I hope that the others will still like me and not resent taking orders."
   c) "I wonder if I really deserved/can do the job?"
2. An event comes to town—concert/sporting event/theatre/lecture—that you'd really like to attend, but no one is available to go with you. You
   a) Buy the best seat and go alone.
   b) Call around until you find *someone,* even your snot-nosed nephew, to accompany you.
   c) Decide it's not going to be fun to go alone and stay home.
3. You meet a delightful someone of the opposite sex and are carried away and spend the night together. He/she doesn't call the next week, and when you call is rather vague about getting together again. You
   a) Keep right on with your own activities, happy to have had a fun night, expecting no more.
   b) Try to figure out what you did wrong.
   c) Are devastated and feel really rejected.
4. When you imagine the future you think
   a) Things will just keep getting better because you're working on it all the time.
   b) Life is pretty much a Mexican stand-off—win a little, lose a little.

   c) There's nothing much the future has to offer you.

5. The last time you did something new and exciting was
   a) Within the last few days.
   b) Not recently, maybe last year's vacation.
   c) It's been so long you can't remember.

6. Saturday night rolls around and you don't have a date. You
   a) Are glad for the respite; it's nice to spend an evening alone doing just what pleases you.
   b) Mope around for a while and then decide to go out anyway, maybe have a drink at the local pub.
   c) Are plunged down in the dumps and do a total review of what a loser you are.

7. Someone you don't know well compliments you on how good you're looking today. Your response is
   a) "Thanks! I appreciate your noticing."
   b) "Oh, this old thing? I've had it for years."
   c) "Must be something wrong with that person's eyesight, or else they want something from me."

8. A holiday weekend is coming up. Everyone you know has plans to go skiing or camping or something. You feel
   a) You can make your own plans independently of others.
   b) Upset because no one included you in their plans so you hint around for an invitation.
   c) Angry and rejected and think of all the lousy friends you have.

9. You go shopping for a major purchase, like a coat. Trying one on that you aren't sure suits you, the salesperson says, "Oh, you should get that one—it's terrific on you." You
   a) Thank him/her for the opinion but say you haven't quite made up your own mind yet.

    b) Think she/he knows better than you and are seri-
       ously tempted to buy the coat.
    c) Make up your mind to take it at once.
10.   You take your lover to meet your family. You are
    a) Fairly sure they will like him/her, but it won't
       matter to the relationship one way or the other.
    b) Quite anxious that they might not approve of your
       choice and wonder how you'll explain.
    c) Absolutely convinced they won't approve—they
       never have before.

How to score yourself: Take three points for every *a,*
two points for *b,* and one point for *c.*

21 to 30—You're independent and gutsy with a high
level of self-esteem. Naturally, the higher your score the
more self-esteem you have. Check your *b* and *c* answers
for the areas you need to be aware of and to work on.

12 to 21—You dither a lot but still manage to come up
with the right decisions some of the time. Trouble is you
are lacking in self-confidence and it's a struggle. You need
to build self-esteem and take more risks.

0 to 12—Your self-esteem is in pretty bad shape. You
tend to let other people do your thinking and deciding for
you, rely on their opinions, and be a downer to yourself.
Never fear, there's always hope. Dig down to that good
person inside and let him/her come up to the surface. One
day you'll realize that your opinion of you is the only one
that matters!

If you checked *c* on question #6, I'd like especially to
say an encouraging word to you. In fact, I'd like you to
skip over to page 209 and read what I have to say about
the Saturday-night date there. Too many people, and this
affects men as well as women, think there's something
magical about Saturday night. But it can be a danger area
for those with low self-esteem; some people, even if they
have had dates Tuesday, Thursday and Friday will still feel

left out of life if they face a Saturday night alone. Remember: *Saturday is no different from any other night of the week*. One sophisticated woman I know actually *refuses* to go out on Saturday! Too crowded, long lines for movies, indifferent service from busy waiters, no taxis, etc. All the days of the week are good days, and each one is an important day in your life. Make the best of each one as it comes along. Don't lay the burden of your self-esteem, or the value of a whole week, on poor Saturday night!

The big first step in building up low self-esteem is to evaluate correctly what you have to work with. Then take action. I've already discussed the many ways you can fix almost anything you think is wrong with you, with the proper attention (unless you're a hardened criminal, that is).

Getting stuck in what I've been referring to as the media-image syndrome is about the worst thing you can do if you have low self-esteem. Remember that real flesh-and-blood functions on reality, not fantasy. This is a point I can't emphasize more strongly. We are all assaulted daily from screen, TV, video, and the print media with the "beautiful people." We never consider that these pictures we see have taken hours and hours to produce—and that with the assistance of a dozen or more helpers. I recently went for a photo session—and it was more work than my normal two jobs of hosting my TV show and answering questions on radio live for three hours each week night! There were make-up artists, hairdressers, clothes stylists, photographer's assistants responsible for complicated lighting, and a host of others, whose jobs I could only guess at, running around the photographers studio. My point is that those beautiful people you see in magazine fashion pictures and on TV didn't just get up out of bed that morning looking that way! They've been primed and painted, posed and lighted, arranged and rearranged to get that effect.

Not long ago, a women's magazine (*Self* magazine, June 1987) made the intelligent comment in an article on swimsuits that if you "fixate" on someone like a bathing-suit model you may "throw in the beach towel." Their succinct comment was: "malarkey," and they proceeded to show some real women wearing the same suit which fit each one differently. A fashion model does not buy—and expect a perfect fit—something "off the rack"; that garment has been pinned and glued, snipped and tacked by an expert fitter to get that sleek look that looks (and is) so impossible for real people to achieve.

So don't, *please don't*, compare yourself to what you see in the images. Kick the media-image-syndrome, and kick it *hard*.

Wearing masks doesn't do much for self-esteem, either. Instead, work on genuine accomplishments and attributes—and soon you'll be much more confident and secure!

Though the next few paragraphs apply especially to my female readers, I want you men to read them just as carefully . . .

There's a brand of thinking still being preached today telling women that their priority in life is to "get" a man. The implication here is that men, like wild animals (or sometimes just grubby little boys) must be trapped into giving up their freedom. One headline of a review about a guide to meeting men that I read said: "Where to spot him, how to *snare* him."

Do I hear you laughing? Well, believe it or not this thinking is still going on. Today's woman is barraged with the statistics of the "Great American Male Shortage." Stories about all the dastardly men whose main mission in life is to sidestep marriage and disappoint women's legitimate desires for wifehood abound. Tales of "the man that got away" are everywhere.

Why?

Because a woman is not supposed to be an independent human being. Here's where the "I'm nothing without a man" philosophy really comes into play. A woman must do whatever is necessary to get a man, including pretending to be what she is not—for life, if need be. Only, of course, no one can pretend for life. If anyone could, the divorce rate would not be standing at a staggering fifty percent.

Why should this be? We've just gone through two generations labeled "Sexual Revolution" and "Women's Liberation," and yet the idea grinds on, burrowing its way deeper and deeper into the consciousness of *both* sexes. Ah—the elusive male!

And, too often, in her frantic attempts to "trap" a man, as she scrambles to conceal her blemishes or her fat thighs, she covers up something else as well: her individuality. Her brains. Her courage. Her creativity.

Now, *that's* sad.

After a bit of discussion, we agreed on a simple principle to guide both men and women over this thorny thicket.

Treat your lover as you would your best friend. No better, no worse. The old Golden Rule still applies: Do Unto Others As You Would Have Them Do Unto You. If you'd appreciate the thoughtfulness of someone having your favorite drink in the house, provide his fixin's, but let *him* do the mixing. Any woman who voluntarily turns herself into a servant to get or keep a man is only short-changing herself.

Whatever your age, let me say here, straight out, that if you are a woman and you think or have been led to believe that you must have a man in your life, and that the only way you can do this is to flatter him, surrender your own personality and bend your entire life to pleasing him, you are headed for a sad time and hard bumps. And, boy, do a lot of women do this!

And if you are a man who has somehow absorbed the

information that this is the only proper way for a woman to behave, that femininity is embodied in self-effacing subservience, you are going to miss out on one of life's great experiences—that of relating to a real human being who is also a woman, grown up, with her own strengths.

I want to tell you about the special place in the woods where the famous lovers Tristan and Isolde went to consummate their love, a sacred grotto.

It was circular, because Love cannot abide in corners. It was white, the color of Integrity. Its floor was green marble, for marble is Constancy and that is always green. There was no lock on the outside, because the need for a lock signifies Treachery. Only those admitted from within can be said truly to Love. Otherwise, it is Deceit or Force. There was a little latch of tin, for Gentleness, and a lever of gold, for Success.

You might consider these ideas when you are building your house of love.

SALLY'S BASIC RULE

Be honest with yourself about who you *truly* are. Then be honest with the other person about what you want. *That's* the way to avoid problems.

Not only do you have a responsibility to be honest with yourself, but intelligent self-protection requires you check out the honesty of someone in whom you're interested.

It takes time. Watch your partner's actions. Listen to his/her words. Keep on the alert for signals that tell you what's *really* going on. And don't try to ignore the signals your antennae are picking up. How many times did something go wrong and you had to admit to yourself you knew it all along? *Be aware.*

Another good checkpoint for a new partner is your friends. Some people are reluctant to introduce a new lover to friends because they are afraid the friends won't like or approve of him/her. That's nonsense. Your friends are your friends. Let them meet your prospective mate. Ask for their frank opinion. A person who is being insincere usually can't convince those who are uninvolved. They are more likely to be objective than you can be when you're caught up in the throes of a new love affair.

That doesn't mean your friends have to fall in love with your lover—only you need to do that. But it can help clarify your own perspective until the results are in.

With honesty, self-confidence, high self-esteem, and just a soupçon of healthy caution, you'll be *glad* that character counts!

10

What About Money?

NOTHING—NOT EVEN religion or politics—is as likely to stimulate controversy as money. What ought to be a simple medium of exchange for goods and services consistently becomes loaded with emotional freight. Projections of all kinds of other problems are stacked onto money's back. Instead of a matter of *money,* it can become, "Does he/she love me?" determined by the amount spent on evenings out and presents. Or, "What will the neighbors think?" determined by how new the car is, how expensive the furniture, how shiny the kids' bicycles. What we spend—upon ourselves, our necessities, our luxuries, our families, our friends, entertaining, social life, vacations—often has a lot more to do with our view of money as a gauge of success than it does with the items purchased.

Many people's money priorities are as muddled as their love priorities. More divorces are caused by disputes about how to handle mutual finances than over sexual incompatibility or infidelity. Money even influences the bedroom. An unfaithful husband may buy his wife a fur coat. An angry wife may go out and run up charge account bills to punish her husband.

Spending money on someone functions as *proof* of love. Flowers and lingerie on Valentine's Day, cameras and jackets on Father's Day, are better evidence of affection than a thousand sonnets. Even children equate love and money. Those who don't feel loved may steal or turn to shoplifting. Youngsters vie for status with one another, using the amount of available pocket money, the latest electronic gadget, or fancy vacations (which, in turn, prove their parents' love). Mommy may buy little Bobby a new firetruck because she feels guilty about the unfair way she screamed at him this morning. Bobby may be confused, because he asked for that firetruck for Christmas and was told Mommy couldn't afford it. Now she can. It must mean she loves him, right?

Money management remains a mystery to many people— especially women, who have been taught that they "mustn't bother their pretty heads" with financial matters. I know a woman of forty, with four children, who wouldn't dream of asking her husband how much he makes. Imagine what would happen if this woman were suddenly at the financial helm of her young family!

I can't tell you how to manage your income, but I understand how complicated the subject of money can be, and I've given some hard thought to how we spend our money in relation to finding love.

High on the priority list is where you live. After all, it's a safe bet you'll be looking for love there, right? I know people who will live in an undesirable neighborhood and then buy a car so they can get out of it. *Wrong*. Spend the money on *where* you live and take the bus. If you want to meet your type of people it's important to live in your type of neighborhood.

A number of my callers have complained that in their neighborhood there's just nobody to meet. Nobody *nice*. So, I ask, why do they live there? They usually give three reasons:

"It's where my family lives."

"It's convenient to my job."

"I'm just out of college and it's all I can afford."

Nonsense.

Let's take these one by one:

If you're not ready to leave your family, you may not be ready to find love. Loving requires independence, and no matter how close your family ties, they must be subordinate to your own life or you'll never find love. Finding love is starting a new family unit.

Your job is important, no doubt about it; but unless you work in some terribly remote spot or are an explorer of the Arctic Circle, chances are you can find nicer accommodations within a reasonably comfortable distance. So what if you have to drive an extra fifteen minutes to get to work? Isn't finding love worth it?

The last is perhaps the most legitimate, but even the newly graduated college person can find living space in a good area. Today many people are choosing to double up or live in groups in order to afford a better apartment or house in a better neighborhood. Not only is this a good way to upgrade where you live, it also brings new people into your life. Roommates have friends and interests you can share.

My father was in the real estate business, and he gave me this advice: take the worst house (or apartment) on the best street. *Never* do the opposite. Some people remain in deteriorating neighborhoods because they have a nice house or apartment there. This is self-defeating, not only in terms of meeting people—it's demoralizing to come home to a rotten neighborhood, where you might not even feel safe.

As long as you remain within the economically prescribed one-quarter to one-third of your income, you should find the best possible home for yourself.

I'm going to digress for a moment because I want to bring up a very important issue.

It's called *putting your life on hold*. Many people are waiting for love to come into their lives before they start living. They wait and wait, thinking tomorrow never comes. But it does. All of those tomorrows are your life. If you put your life on hold while waiting for love to come and change it for you, you are making a serious mistake.

"Oh, there's no sense getting a better apartment because when I get married I'll be moving anyway." *Wrong*.

Get the best you can afford *now*. The best way to find love is to be living your life to the fullest *all the time*.

So what if you have to move? You'd move if you got a better job in another state, wouldn't you? But do you want to sit around and wait until that job offer pops up? Of course not!

That doesn't mean you have to go out and spend a fortune either. The nice thing about apartments and houses is that they don't need to be crammed full of furniture. Empty spaces are appealing. You can live with little in the way of furnishings and decoration. Less is better. Big fluffy cushions sometimes can take the place of sofas and chairs. The Japanese look is very popular and functional; simplicity at its best. Decorate with plants. They are an inexpensive way to bring charm, warmth, and the sense of life into a room.

My friend Sarah has a one-room studio apartment on a really good block in Manhattan. It's a bit more than she can afford, but it's light and airy—and she loves coming home to a tree-lined street.

She painted the walls and floor bright shiny white, and mirrored one wall with stick-on panels from the dime store. Her double-sized mattress went right on the newly painted floor, covered with a fluffy quilt she got at a white sale. She stitched up some brightly colored pillows to toss on the mattress, added a beanbag chair she found at a garage sale in the country. Then she bought a huge palm tree and several plants and scattered them around the room.

The result? It's one of the most delightfully peaceful places I know to visit.

Cars are another issue. Like money, they have taken on an inflated role in our society. Psychologists point out that cars have become an extension of our egos. Some people practically live in their cars, as a snail carries its house on its back.

I want to tell you a secret. The very rich, the ones with ''old money'' drive awful cars. They have one requirement of a car: that it can go. It's not a way of showing how much money they make. It's not a way of advertising how sexy they are. A car is not there to make a public statement about you. It is there to get you where you want to go.

The next item on my list is *leather*. Really good leather is the mark of a discriminating person. Whether it's shoes, handbags, briefcases, wallets or a great jacket, leather says *class*. Yes, it is an investment—but a *good* leather item will outlast half a dozen cheap ones. And all you men out there . . . no matter what business you're in, your leather makes the statement that you're serious.

If you absolutely cannot afford the real thing, don't resort to cheap or fake leather. Go for a natural fabric. There are plenty of lovely woven purses and stylish canvas briefcases available. *Replace anything shabby*—whether it be your wallet or your shoes or sneakers. ''Down at the heels'' looks pretty dreadful to anyone.

On the other hand, have all the *fake* jewelry you want, as long as it is of good quality. With the real stuff so vulnerable to being snatched, it's wise to have imitations of excellent taste and quality.

One exception—if you like real gold, one piece that has special meaning for you can become your signature. Personally, I don't like a lot of jewelry on men, but a man might have a gold watch inherited from his father or grandfather, or a signet or class ring. A woman I know has a single gold bangle that she bought to celebrate her thirtieth birthday. No matter what other jewelry she wears, she always wears that bracelet. Fannie Hurst wore a single gold calla lily pin at all times. That was *her* signature.

What I said about cars applies to jewelry—you don't wear it to show how much money you make or to make a statement about your ego. Jewelry is to enhance your appearance and your mood.

Social clubs can offer excellent ways for meeting new people. For those of you living in suburban areas or small-to medium-sized cities, think of joining your local country/golf/tennis club. The best way to identify the right club *for you* is to ask others. Here's a call I answered on this question.

CAROLE: Hi Sally, How are you?

SALLY: Fine. How are you?

CAROLE: Well, I m okay, but I've got a problem and I need your advice.

SALLY: Shoot. That's what I'm here for.

CAROLE: I've just got a new job.

SALLY: That's a problem? (Carole laughs)

CAROLE: No, that's not a problem. It's a neat job. I'm an assistant buyer in a department store.

SALLY: Okay.

CAROLE: It's that I had to move here to Dallas from my home in Grand Rapids and I don't know anybody and I don't know how to go about meeting people I think I'd like.

SALLY: How did you meet people in Grand Rapids?

CAROLE: Mostly at the country club my parents belong to. It wasn't fancy or anything like that. But we had a good time.

SALLY: What did you do?

CAROLE: Oh, we swam, and danced, and hung out. They

had open socials—you know, parties where you could bring guests who didn't belong to the club. We even had tea dances in the summer on the terrace.

SALLY: Sounds nice. Why don't you join a country club in Dallas?

CAROLE: Well, like I said I don't know anyone. You have to have an introduction or a recommendation.

SALLY: Okay, here's what you do. You go to your boss—if you have more than one, pick the one you like best. You go in with a prepared compliment. Tell her how comfortable she's made you feel, or how well you think she runs the department, or whatever sounds right to you. Don't lie, though; she'll see through it. Find something you can honestly compliment her on.

At that point she's going to beam in your direction and ask if there's anything she can do to help you, or she'll ask how you are doing in your job, or something.

So far, so good. You say the job is going well but that you really miss your swimming, or golf, or tennis, and that you don't know where to go, that you'd like to join a club. Or just say you're a country-club-type person and you'd like to join one for the social life. Ask her for a recommendation, for the name of a club that might suit your style. Obviously, if you're thirty you don't want to go to the oldest, most staid, traditional club in town where the youngest member turned seventy last week.

Talk a little bit about what you like, mention that your parents belonged to a club at home and what you did there. Tell her you like a relaxed, leisurely atmosphere.

CAROLE: Okay. I can do that.

SALLY: Fine. If she herself doesn't belong to a club, she will know someone who does or who can advise. Then invite that person out for a drink—remember, you pay— and ask them to tell you about their club. Be charming and be yourself. By the time the drink and chat have finished, you should have a recommendation, or whatever is needed for membership.

CAROLE: That sounds like a good plan.

SALLY: It's always good to ask people for specific things. Never be vague. Usually people are quite happy to help if they are told something specific they can do for you. Just to complain about not having a social life wouldn't do anything. But if you can ask for something specific on a nondemanding basis, chances are good you'll get a positive response. Most of us like to help others out when we can.

CAROLE: Thanks, Sally. That's a real help.

SALLY: Good talking to you.

The same process holds true for any organization you might be interested in. Welcome Wagon and the Newcomers Club provide information to newcomers. Again, do your research. Find out if Club A is for the old fogies and, if Club B is for the young marrieds, Club C might be the one for you.

The questionnaire that you filled out at the beginning of this section, "What's Your Style?," will help you get a handle on how to proceed.

If a church or temple is your style, ask around to find out which ones would be the most compatible to you and most likely to attract the kind of people you want to meet. Churches are really good places for singles to meet; many have a full social calendar and sponsor events and trips. Church- or temple-sponsored activities are often modestly priced, and they sometimes have group rates for theater tickets and the like.

Health and fitness clubs are also a good bet—though some of them can be quite pricey. Still, especially for the city dweller, they can be super avenues for meeting new people. A clear advantage (over, say, the bar scene) is that you are not only meeting people who share your interests in keeping fit but you are. *doing something for yourself*. This is an automatic conversation-opener. All you need to do is stroll over to whomever strikes your fancy and ask a question about the club's facilities and you're off and running! (Conversationally, that is.)

Again, ask around to find out which club most suits your style and temperament. Check into the co-ed activities first. Try to chat with some current members.

Last but not least on the roster of allocating money to find love comes your *vacation*. Vacation times are wonderful opportunities to meet romance, and not just for the short term. Don't be stopped by the idea that if you meet someone on vacation it's doomed to be only a "summer romance." My friend Alice met her man while she was sitting in a swimming pool up at a Finger Lakes resort. He was Canadian, but he was planning to move to New York. Now they're happily married. So *save* for that vacation! It's one of your best bets for finding love.

What if you want to meet a rich person and you're not rich? Where are they? First, learn to "think rich." Take polo matches. Everyone knows that only the rich can afford to play polo, right? But anyone can *watch* a polo match! There's usually not even a gate fee. People go in their cars and park round the field. No one is going to check your bank account at a polo match. Later on, I'll go into specifics about where to go to find the rich, but my point here is that rich is a state of mind first. There are millionaires who never feel as if they have enough money because they are still hugging their nursery insecurities. And there are free spirits without a dime and without a care who think they own the earth just because the sun is shining. It's all in how you look at it.

11

Is Age a Factor?

CONNIE: Sally, my problem is that I'm forty-one and my boyfriend is twenty-nine.

SALLY: Why is that a problem?

CONNIE: Well, he's younger than I am.

SALLY: I can tell that, but what's the problem?

CONNIE: My friends think it's ridiculous for a woman my age to be involved with a man so much younger.

SALLY: Are you happy with him?

CONNIE: Yes. I really like him. He's a terrific lover and a really nice person.

SALLY: Is he happy with you?

CONNIE: Oh, yes. He compliments me all the time, tells me I'm beautiful and sexy, and loves my cooking.

SALLY: You still haven't told me the problem.

CONNIE: It's my age. His age. I mean, the differences in our ages.

SALLY: What difference does the difference in your ages make if you're both happy? Do you have things to talk about?

CONNIE: My goodness, we *never* stop talking! We just talk about anything and everything.

143

SALLY: Do you laugh together?

CONNIE: All the time. He's very witty and I just seem to set him off.

SALLY: All right. It sounds like a pretty good relationship to me.

CONNIE: Oh, it is!

SALLY: But you said you had a problem.

CONNIE: It's my friends and family. They don't think I ought to be with him. Because he's so much younger.

SALLY: What does he think?

CONNIE: He thinks I shouldn't listen to them.

SALLY: He's right! You've got a good man there. Hang onto him.

CONNIE: But what about the age difference?

SALLY: Forget it. It doesn't matter. What matters is the quality of the relationship.

I get a lot of calls like this. All over America people are worried about age, and not just about being too *old*. Some even worry about being too young, if you can imagine that!

Is age a factor?

A lot of the worry about age—especially female—is fueled by the depressing statistics on the male/female ratio being tossed around. According to estimates from the 1980 census, there are approximately 30 million single women vying for 21.5 million men. Whew!

In the up-to-age-thirty group, there is a surplus of men. Good news.

In the thirty to thirty-five group, there are 102 women for every 100 men. Not so bad.

As you get older, the news gets worse. From thirty-five to forty, there are only 100 men for every 128 women.

Women over fifty, or so they say, can forget the whole ballgame.

Now, let me tell you about my Aunt Carrie. She's a lady to be reckoned with, by anyone's standards. Aunt Carrie married five times. The third time she was forty-two and met her husband at a singles bar in New York. The fifth (and she hopes last) time, she was sixty-two and her husband was fifty.

Time magazine ran a squib recently about a well-known actress. She married for the third time at seventy-two. Her husband was sixty. Her third, his *first*. Mary Tyler Moore, at forty-five, has married a man of thirty. And Olivia Newton-John, at thirty-eight, married Matt Lattanzi, aged twenty-eight.

And celebrity couples aren't the only ones where a woman marries a younger man. Let me tell you a story. For my television show, I interviewed a number of couples whose age differences were fairly substantial—there were the traditional older man–younger woman couples as well as the less traditional older woman–younger man arrangement.

In this case, the man is thirty years old and his wife is fifty-five. She's a rather glamorous lady, well-groomed and chic, with enough money to travel well. One year she took a trip to Israel on a top-of-the-line tour, and her travel agent put her in touch with an Israeli tour guide.

Now, tour guides are quite common in Europe and countries that attract tourists, even though we don't have them so much in America. He was multi-lingual, very debonair and sophisticated, nice-looking with a full beard, very competent and skilled at handling people. They became involved.

When she first returned home from her trip, she chalked it up to a summer romance, but *he* was burning up the transatlantic phone lines and she realized that this might be something deeper than a fling.

Five months later, she made another trip to Israel, and it was then she discovered the twenty-five-year age difference. Given his sophistication and appearance, it came as something of a shock to her. Thirty and fifty-five? Impossible. (She's a fairly conservative sort.) Nonetheless, her lover reassured her that he didn't give a damn how old she was.

She gave it a six-months' trial. They lived together in Israel. It worked, and she forgot traditional thinking about "proper" age differences between men and women.

At first her children were aghast and she was worried, but after meeting him they cast aside their prejudices and cheered her on.

An extraordinarily handsome and happy couple, they have been married for four years.

Take Howard and Jane. They are in the older man–younger woman category. Jane was a sales manager for a major soft drink company based in Los Angeles, and then her company transferred her to St. Louis. The first day she was out in a suburban area looking for an apartment. She was well-dressed, wearing a suit trimly tailored, and looking her best. It had snowed the night before and, being from the West Coast, she didn't have proper cold-weather wear, so she was tottering down the middle of the street (which had been cleared of snow) in her high heels. A man, jogging, approached her. Since she wasn't warmly dressed, he could tell that she was looking for an apartment, and he said there was one vacant in his building and offered to show her his.

Quite naturally, she was a bit cautious about going to a strange man's apartment. He looked perfectly safe, but prudence told her to say, "No, thank you." But she did go as far as the hall of the building to have a look. He offered to contact the building's management on the following day and check into the vacancy for her. She thanked him, giving him her business card and telling him the name of her hotel. He mentioned that her hotel was across the street from his office, and they parted.

The following day he called and left a message with the information about the apartment. A couple of days later he decided to nip across the street for a drink at the hotel bar. He remembered the nice lady he'd helped and decided to ring her room. She had just washed her hair, but he insisted that he didn't care a fig how she looked—just come on down and have a drink, he said.

Jane went, almost on a whim, because he had been so nice and, after all, she knew no one in St. Louis except her colleagues at work. She half-dried her hair and pinned it up under a pretty scarf, put on new make-up, and donned a simple but elegant woolen jersey dress. She particularly remembers the dress because of its color—red—and the fact that it was her only winter dress. She'd bought it just the day before.

She had a couple of drinks with him that evening. Later, they started to date. A couple of weeks into it, he said to her one evening over dinner, "You know I'm old enough to be your father." (At the time, he was 60 and she was 35.)

She wouldn't believe it. He was in great physical shape and looked no more than forty-five.

The curious thing about mature people is that they all begin to look about the same age. At thirty-five, she could have been forty-five, not because of wrinkles but because of the confident way she handled herself. At sixty, he could have been anywhere from forty-five to fifty-five.

Jane and her jogger friend have been happily married for seven years.

Where did she find him? Walking down the middle of the street.

Was she looking her best? Even though she wasn't expecting to encounter anyone that morning except a rental agent, she was.

Was she brave enough to talk to a strange man?
Yes, she was. And her self-esteem helped her over the

stumbling block of not having her hair "done," so that she could accept his first invitation.

Was he ready to find love?

The answer is obvious. Even jogging in the snow.

Was he honest and up front about himself?

He'd never lied about his age, and when their relationship began to look as though it could become serious, he told her the facts.

Did he let the age difference deter him?

He weighed the pros and cons, decided it was okay with him, that he could handle it, and then let it be a mutual decision.

The result? *A happy ending!* So forget about all the statistics and concentrate on you!

Is age a factor?

Of course it is. But so is everything else!

I'll grant you that these stories aren't the everyday case, but they've worked. I think that we've all bought a bill of goods on the age issue, but women, especially, seem to subscribe to this formula thinking. Well, never mind what you have been hearing about the discrepancy in the ratio of men to women—the numbers aren't the whole story. I say forget the numbers. You need only one person. All in all, female callers are usually afraid to consider a man even a *few years younger,* let alone twenty or thirty.

I would like to wave a big red flag right under their noses and say, "Look around!" There are plenty of men out there who are available if you don't put on age-related blinkers. Forget what other people think! Think what *you* think. Society is going to have to change, but I can't do that alone, so you're going to have to help. Each one who shakes off the stereotype adds a brick to the new building of social reform.

Another thing to consider: the male-female ratio is going to change (already has) with the younger generations. In a few years, according to the demographics, there are probably going to be many, many more men than women—and then where will those young men go to find women if not to older women? I want women to know that it is *okay* to be with a younger man.

So, if you're a woman and you're concerned with an age difference, then you are really more concerned about what people will think than you are about creating your own personal happiness. And that doesn't say much for your priorities, does it?

You've heard that a great many men who are approaching what has been called "male menopause," which occurs around ages thirty-seven to forty, go out to seek a much younger woman to bolster their sagging self-images. Instead of welcoming their maturity, they panic. A young girl on their arm and in their bed may make them feel, for a brief moment anyway, that time is not a-flyin' quite so quickly. But these men may eventually learn that the youngest nymphet cannot still the hands of time, and in the meantime, they have wasted time, energy, and often quite a bit of money chasing a fantasy. The opportunity for a solid relationship with the joy and comfort that a mature woman can bring may have passed them by—and sometimes, indeed, it is too late.

Listen to this story from one caller of mine about his efforts to stop the clock.

Jim was forty-two, had married young, and had recently divorced after twenty years of marriage. Released from his home-wife-family-kids life into the world of singles, he went a bit wild. He scooped up as many young beauties as time and energy would allow, perhaps making up a bit for the lost youth he had spent in his marriage. At first it was a heady business—he was successful and could afford to wine and dine his young dates, one as young as nineteen, barely older than his oldest daughter.

But gradually he found that he and these nubile ladies

really didn't have too much to talk about, and he began
to yearn for a female contemporary. He moved up in the
age bracket until he was dating women in their thirties.
Eventually, that soured and he turned to his own genera-
tion—ladies in their forties. Well, that didn't work too
well either. But one night he met a woman of fifty-two,
and he found himself fascinated.

This is how *he* tells it:

Women in their twenties intimidated him with their rush
to immediate sex. He was brought up on older values and
couldn't handle it comfortably.

Women in their thirties, especially the later thirties,
seemed to him over-anxious to marry in order not to miss
having children. He already *had* children, and didn't want
any more.

Women in their forties were in more or less the same
boat as himself, with one exception—many had returned to
the work force late and were concentrating on their careers.

Then *voila!* Jim discovered women in their fifties.

"Women in their fifties are relaxed and comfortable
with themselves. They've had their children and enough
experience to be understanding and compassionate. Sexually, they know what they want and that makes it easier,
but they're not determined to get a man in bed on the first
date."

I only wish there were more men like Jim. Instead of
barking up the tree of extreme youth for the fleeting
pleasures of illusion, they could be getting some real
satisfaction and understanding in a relatively problem-free
relationship.

But, it's the *women* who have the hardest time adjusting
to age differences. Unfortunately, they've bought that old
cultural bug-a-boo that a man *has* to be older (and, equally
nonsensically, taller, wiser, and richer) than a woman. If I
can get one message across to my women readers, especially those over 30, it is FORGET ABOUT AGE. Stop

considering it. Stop discussing it. People get more hung up on this one topic than any other, and I hear it night after night as I answer calls on ABC Radio network. *Please, please*, for your own good and everybody else's, stop fastening on AGE, as if it were some dreadful incurable disease. Relationships work or they don't work, and that's a fact. But age is not what determines if a relationship will work or continue to work.

Society may still frown on an older woman married to a younger man, but society is changing. And you can help it to change more by not getting fixated on age. If it's perfectly all right for a *man* to have a wife 20 or even 30 years younger—then what's the difference if a *woman* has a younger husband? None at all. It's all in the mind. Change your attitude, change and improve your chance of finding love. The well-known Dr. Joyce Brothers has commented that "Age, unless you are teenagers, for normal people is not all that prominent." What is important is what people have in common and how they care about each other. Sometimes, of course, a woman who is older will be more experienced, wiser, but if she is she'll have the sense to use her advantage well, and she will learn from her younger lover just as much as he can learn from her. Each age level adds something to the other, in bed and out.

Older women are able to make sexual contact easier and more stimulating for a man, because of their years of experience, and certainly younger men bring a wonderful *joie de vivre* to the bedroom with their sheer enthusiasm. They haven't seen/done it all—there's still a lot of territory to explore sexually. Of course, there are no guarantees of happiness—as many a couple of similar age and background have discovered sadly in the divorce courts. But when love walks in, preconceived notions about what is "right" (as in age differences) and what is "wrong" just seem to fade away. So, don't stand in your own way. Refuse to let those old age shibboleths dictate to you. You're in charge of your own life. Don't you forget it!

Is age a factor?

There is one time, and one time only, when age is a *determining* factor, and that is when biological children are a factor. It is no good for a woman past childbearing years to enter into a relationship with a man of thirty who wants a family of his own (unless, of course, they agree to adopt). Similarly, there's difficulty ahead in a marriage between a man of sixty-five and a woman of childbearing age who wants biological children.

But these are the exceptions. In general, I suggest you follow:

SALLY'S BASIC RULE

Age shouldn't even be considered. Date and marry anyone of any age unless reproduction is a consideration. No matter what your sex, if someone asks your age, field the question. (There's always time to answer later, when it won't matter.)

So, if a man asks a woman her age, she can answer with a charming enigmatic smile, even if she's ten years younger, and say, "I'm as old as you want me to be," or "I'm ageless, can't you tell?"

If a woman asks a man his age, he can look directly into her eyes and say nothing. Or he can say, "I'm as old as you are," or "I'm at my most interesting age."

A question about age is an invasion of privacy and an attempt to stereotype. Fight back! The big problem about age as I see it is that, like money, it becomes loaded with emotional freight, a way of *categorizing*. We hear about a new person and right away ask, "How old is he/she?" —not because we're genuinely interested, but because it's a way of pigeonholing the person. That's what I'm trying to get all of you *not* to do. Don't force others into categories, no matter how convenient it may seem. You are bound to miss a lot if you do. And when you're out there looking for love, don't let yourself be categorized either.

I'd like to take a moment to tell you about a curious twist on the May-December romance stereotype. Nowadays, when it's the man who's older, he's almost embarrassed—rather than smug—to be seen with a nymphet. A lot of people stare. A man I know with a much younger girl friend told me, "I can't take her anywhere. It's unbearable. Everybody looks at me as if I'm playing daddy to this young woman, as if I've lost my mind. I have to hide her, keep her a secret."

A survey I read recently made the point that women of comparable age dislike seeing older men with much younger women.

So, if nowadays a man's friends lecture him on the unsuitability of his choice of a much younger woman, the tables are turning. But this is no good either. We need freedom, all of us, to move up and down the ladder of age as we see fit. It's hard enough to find anyone with whom you have enough in common to have a serious, long-term relationship—letting age complicate the matter further is just plain silly.

Is age a factor?
Don't let it be!
We all have limitations enough without adding the age factor to the list. The purpose is to be yourself, and to be the best self you can, and not to let anyone stick a label on you that will in any way limit your opportunities to find love. Don't you stick a label on anyone else either!

Besides, what you really want is someone who is *interesting*, right? No matter what age. So let's get on and talk about what makes people interesting to themselves and to each other.

12

Do Interests Pay Dividends?

Indubitably, as the fabled Jimmy Durante used to say. To *find* an interesting person, you have to *be* an interesting person. This is a truism. Interesting people look for other interesting people.

If the last, most interesting thing you did was going to your Aunt Tillie's golden anniversary or getting caught in a rainstorm while walking your dog, or if your conversation is limited to what was on TV last night or that incipient pimple you fear is hatching, you aren't exactly going to sparkle.

Let's face it, the prettiest girl or the most glamorous woman, the best-looking young hunk or the handsomest man, isn't going to make romantic hay if other people start yawning when he/she opens his/her mouth!

The most attractive rampant narcissist, no matter how physically attractive, who can only talk about him/herself, will have people fleeing in droves. A famous philosopher defined the bore as "Someone who deprives me of my solitude without providing companionship."

The person who can't carry on an interesting conversation is going to be a social failure. The ability to *contribute*

155

something interesting to others fertilizes the soil of romantic possibility.

How many times have you said or heard it said that, "so-and-so is such an *interesting* person." Maybe you've wished you could be more like so-and-so. Well, it's very easy to correct the problem. Almost every one of us is interested in *something* (besides ourselves, that is!).

In this chapter I'm going to help you define and expand your interests because, yes, interests do pay dividends. Interests allow you to express yourself in ways that your jobs, friends, and family do not. They help you find out who you truly are. Not only can they be fun and exciting in themselves, but they are major pathways to expanding anyone's social life.

I confess that I am *appalled* at the number of calls I get from people who don't have hobbies! If you listen to my show, you know I've got them by the dozen. In fact, there's very little that doesn't interest me, even if I'm not going to pursue it at full tilt. What about you? Are you someone who just goes to work and then comes home and turns on the boob tube for the evening's entertainment? If you are, and I hate to say this, you're going to come off as a very dull person. Unless, of course, you find someone else who has no other interests in life than working to maintain the basic necessities and spending the rest of their time glued to the tube. "Couch potatoes," they're called, and if that's you and you've found another one, then why are you reading this book? You're reading this book because you aren't satisfied with the way things are in your life. You want to *find love*. And to find love, you have to meet new people, and have something to talk to them about.

Meeting people through shared interests is an automatic conversational icebreaker. Whether it's the Green Bay Packers or astrology, already you have something in common to talk about. I remember once I met a fellow who was very nice, all decked out in a three-piece pinstripe suit. He was pleasant enough, and not bad to look at, but he didn't turn me on until I discovered that he had the largest collection of 1920s jazz records in New York City. He knew all about the old musicians, their lives, who made what song famous, and he could tell fascinating stories about the evolution of jazz and its performers. I was enchanted.

Or take my friend Alice. A top-notch executive, she wears Gucci shoes and buys her dresses in the best shops. Her nails are always perfectly manicured. Still, Alice didn't fill her time with much else besides her work. Always an overachiever, she hadn't allowed herself time for much relaxation until the day her doctor discovered she had high blood pressure.

He cautioned her to relax, slow down.

"How?" she asked.

"Find a hobby."

Alice had always loved flowers, so she decided to take a course in flower arranging. She became fascinated by orchids. Learning about the stunningly numerous varieties, she began to think about growing them. She had a little greenhouse built on her Manhattan terrace and began culti- vating the delicate plants. Even in freezing weather, she spent time with her flowers, naming each one as if it were a child.

At thirty-eight, Alice had met mostly men in her profes- sion, men who tended to be high-powered workaholics. She'd dated quite a few, had some affairs, but always ended up either canceling dates or having them canceled because of one or the other's meetings. Shoptalk had begun to bore her completely.

Three years ago, she decided to attend a conference of orchid growers in Miami during her vacation. There, she met Roger, a garden writer with a specialty in orchid culture. Quiet and mild, he seemed as different from Alice as day from night. Alice's orchid hobby was an expression of her own need for respite from the hustle and bustle of business, and Roger's calm manner fit right into that. He writes at home, so there's no conflict with busy schedules. Together, now married, they hover over their plants, discussing the minutiae of their mutual interest.

SALLY'S BASIC RULE

Become an expert at something. It doesn't matter what it is. Discover your own hidden passion, or use what you already know about.

If you can't easily pinpoint an interest, try to think of something you wanted to do when you were a kid, maybe something you forgot you liked. Or, like Alice, turn a passive interest into an active one: if you like looking at pictures, consider learning to draw or take photographs.

Susan met Michael this way. She had liked taking pictures of her cat and decided to expand into photos of pets for an album. Michael was walking his elegant red setter. She asked if she could take the dog's photo, and of course he said yes. Who could resist? The photo session in the park led to coffee, which led to photos of Michael's dog and his two Siamese cats posing together in a charming heap.

Today, Susan includes photographs of the twins she and Michael produced in their second year of marriage, along with the family's assortment of cats and dogs.

The trick is to turn your interest to gold—the gold of a love relationship.

So, put on your thinking cap and consider the possibilities. Here's a list . . .

ART

Interested in great *objets d'art?* No matter where you live, you have plenty of options.

- Museum lectures or courses
- Drawing/painting classes
- Photography
- A particular historical period or individual artist, for example, the French Impressionists, postmodernism, nineteenth-century prints, tapestry, Fabergé, Art Deco, specific artists
- Architecture: walking tours
- Special exhibitions at art galleries
- Antiques: shows
- Auctions

CRAFTS AND HOBBIES

The list is nearly endless, but here are just a few ways you can pursue your creative sides:

- Sewing/needlework/quilting
- Toys: collecting
- Jewelry making
- Flower arranging
- Metalworking
- Puppetry
- Weaving
- Woodworking
- Pottery
- Leatherworking
- Mask-making
- Basket-weaving
- Fly-making (fishing)

ANIMALS

Everybody (well, almost everybody) loves animals. Conversational possibilities between animal lovers are unlimited and rapport is almost guaranteed.

- Dog and cat shows
- Volunteer work with pet shelters
- Photography
- Breeding
- Study of breeds
- Horse racing
- Tropical fish
- Exotic birds
- Unusual pets
- Bird watching

COLLECTING

The shyest person in town will talk about his/her collection of miniature glass birds! And collecting leads to *knowledge*.

- Antiques
- Old quilts
- Glass
- Records
- Nostalgia
- Trivia
- Bottles
- Posters
- Record covers
- Record collecting
- Anything at all!

CULTURAL PURSUITS

Anyone with an active cultural pursuit has a golden opportunity to build a pyramid of interests. A love of music can lead to a study of musical history, a passion for dance brings one into contact with the enthralling lives of dancers, and so forth.

- Opera
- Ballet
- Theater (little theater groups, theater clubs)
- Acting
- Dancing
- Mime
- Clowning
- Concerts (especially outdoor ones)/Jazz clubs
- Movies

ACTIVITIES

The pursuit of any activity will bring you into contact with others who share your interests. Craftspeople gather together at fairs and sell to the public. Wine tastings bring together Beaujolais and Chablis lovers.

- Gardening
- Gourmet cooking and classes
- Wine tasting
- Karate
- Tai-chi
- Flea markets
- Open markets of all sorts
- Fairs (local, crafts, etc.)
- Square dancing

COMMON CAUSES

Many's the marriage made on the campaign trail. There's nothing like the shared interest—and the heat and passion—of a political campaign to show one's mettle, and any deeply felt commitment to a cause is guaranteed to spark intense conversations, the forerunner to romance.

- Political campaigns
- "Save the Whales"
- Save the Anythings
- Community interests
- Volunteer work
- Scouting
- Environmental organizations

INTELLECTUAL PURSUITS

Anyone who can play the piano at a party can take center stage almost immediately. People who *know* about a variety of subjects always have something to say and their self-confidence stays high.

- Foreign languages
- College courses
- Music lessons
- Noncredit courses
- Workshops
- Lectures
- New skills

SPORTS

Besides keeping you fit, they are an excellent way to meet new people and hone self-confidence. If actually playing a sport is not for you, spectator sports are fun for *everyone*.

And a good rousing cheer for the home team might send you into the arms of that nice person sitting next to you in an enthusiastic hug.

- Tennis
- Swimming
- Sailing
- Power boating
- Scuba diving
- Hot air ballooning
- Horseback riding
- Rollerskating
- Ice skating
- Racquetball
- Helicopter flying
- Airplane flying
- Hang-gliding
- Car racing
- Bicycle riding
- Running
- Spectator sports (football, baseball, ice hockey, tennis, basketball, wrestling)
- Skiing
- Mountain climbing.
- Soccer
- Polo

GAMES

For the less strenuously inclined, there are games a-plenty— not only the newest, hot computer ones, but more gentle ones of times past that foster companionship and getting-to-know you evenings.

- Bridge
- Chess
- Darts

- Pool
- Ping-pong
- Cards
- Dominoes
- Board games

OCCULT SUBJECTS

Today, more and more people are interested in astrology, dreams and psychic developments. There are plenty of workshops, lectures and field trips on these subjects, so if you have a leaning toward ESP or would like to learn to interpret your own horoscope, investigate . . .

- Astrology
- Tarot cards
- Psychic development
- UFOs
- ESP
- Dream analysis
- Haunted houses
- Crystals
- Healing
- Anything New Age

TRAVEL

- Anywhere. If you can't go, be an armchair traveler and read about where you would like to go. Travel locally—investigate your own area. Find out all you can about wherever it is that you're going.

   Almost any activity you choose is going to have an organization, possibly its own magazine. Get to know these as ways of being in touch with those who will share your interest.

I've by no means exhausted the possibilities with this list. It's just to get you thinking about the things you might like to do to increase your opportunities for finding love.

Naturally, there are some gender differences to interests. I wouldn't advise that a man wanting to meet women always concentrate on traditional male active sports. He might instead join a gardening club or take a course in needlepoint. Don't laugh till you've tried it. A woman looking for male companionship might consider a course in stockbroking or attend a hockey game. Interestingly, jazz is a great topic for women interested in meeting men. Most jazz clubs are populated heavily by men, and as jazz is not a jock sport, there's plenty of opportunity for appreciative conversation between sets. Remember, though, that jazz buffs are serious listeners. They don't talk while the music is being played. Pursue what pleases you, but if your aim is to expand your romantic opportunities, choose wisely.

Without question, people who are enthusiastic and interested are interesting . . . and they are the ones who attract others easily. Even if you're a rank beginner, if you take the trouble to learn about your sport, cultural interest or whatever, you'll soon find like-minded others.

For example, there's no better place for meeting true opera lovers than the long standing-room lines at New York City's magnificient Metropolitan Opera House. People often arrive in the cold, dark hours of the early morning for a place in line, and camaraderie between them quickly develops. Some go for coffee and bring it to the others. Nobody tries to take anyone else's place in the line. People share the food they have brought. Conversations thrive. The old hands help the newer ones. New friendships bloom.

This is not to say that you and your lover must have identical interests. Insisting that you do is like children who draw a "magic circle" around themselves, enclosing themselves and excluding everyone else.

Couples who seek likeness to the exclusion of differences can be in trouble. Though it is easy enough to fall in love with someone who is—or who seems to be—a reflection of ourselves, there is, I think, a greater value in a balance of opposites and likenesses over the distance of a relationship.

Take Marjorie. She said, "Oh, Sally, I've finally found the *perfect* man! We agree about everything!"

Well, that's nice to begin with, but ultimately it will become boring and stultifying. You may think that because you run, or play tennis, or love concerts, it is vital that the lover in your life share your interest. Ask yourself how often you indulge in any of these activities.

The point about interests is that they make you more interesting! I may not care a hoot about a particular subject, in terms of taking it up, but I can spend an entire evening totally absorbed in someone who loves it and wants to talk to me about it. I never bird-watch, but I once found it fascinating to learn, on a long train ride, all about yellow-tailed and red-spotted and black-beaked feathered friends. And my seat companion, though his favorite drink was bourbon-and-branch-water, found my knowledge of viniculture and wines equally interesting.

Interests are a way of meeting those-like-you; they are also a way of upping your own interest-quotient.

While all interests in common isn't desirable, *no* interests in common, or interests that are too divergent, can tilt the balance the other way. If weekends are your principal source of relaxation, the time you follow your special interest, and it is, say, sailing, you'll be hard-put to live with a confirmed landlubber. What's really important must be shared—and that's up to you to decide.

The problem, usually, isn't too many interests, it's too few. If you have many to choose from and are open to expanding your possibilities, you will find that happy and compatible balance. But if you're not interested in anything, then you're not going to be interesting. You don't want a dull partner, and neither does anyone else.

Take my advice: get up and go out and do something. Get involved. The more interests you have, the more interesting you will become. It might even make a crucial difference as it did with Steve, who called me one night from Brownsville, Texas.

STEVE: Hi, Sally!

SALLY: Hi, there.

STEVE: How's tricks up there in New York? (Said with a wistful twinge)

SALLY: Fine, thanks. How about where you are?

STEVE: Where I am is Brownsville, Texas, and, frankly, it's the pits!

SALLY: (Laughing) What's wrong?

STEVE: Oh, just about everything. I'm in the Army, for one thing. Bored out of my skull for another. And very, very lonely for a lady.

SALLY: Well, I can't help you with being in the Army. I'm not allowed to recommend desertion over the airwaves. But bored and lonely we can talk about.

STEVE: (Unimpressed) Yeah?

SALLY: There's never any reason for being bored. Unless you're bored with yourself. Are you bored with yourself?

STEVE: I guess you might say that. You see, I'm a real New Yorker. Used to the fast life of the city—sports, theatre, all that. There's not much of anything here.

SALLY: Have you really looked?

STEVE: Not too much, I guess. We've got sports enough at the base and I get a lot of exercise—maybe too much. (Laughing)

SALLY: What else do you like to do? You mentioned the theatre. I'm a theatre buff myself, so I know how a theatre person enjoys it.

STEVE: To tell you the truth, it's Broadway I liked—
the lights, the glamour, the kind of people you see
and meet when you're out on the town in the theatre
district.

SALLY: Okay. I understand that. But theatre people are
theatre people wherever.

STEVE: Maybe so, but there's no theatre hereabouts.

SALLY: Have you considered little theatre?

STEVE: What's that?

SALLY: That's local groups that get together and produce
plays for their own enjoyment and whatever audience
they can get.

STEVE: Sounds pretty tame.

SALLY: Why don't you give it a try? What do you have to
lose? There are lots of actors and actresses on Broadway
today who started out in local little theatres.

STEVE: Okay, thanks Sally.

A couple of months later, Steve called me again.

STEVE: Hi, Sally! I'm the guy from Brownsville who was
looking for something to do and you suggested little
theatre. Remember me?

SALLY: Sure I do. How are you doin'?

STEVE: I'm doing fine, just fine. I've found myself a real
cool lady and we are thinking of tying the knot!

SALLY: (Astonished) That's pretty quick work for a man
who was alone a few months ago! How'd you do it?

STEVE: I took your advice. I went out and joined the
Brownsville little theatre and met me the sweetest little
gal you ever saw.

SALLY: (Laughing) You're beginning to sound like a
Texan!

STEVE: It's my girlfriend. We've been acting in a play
together, and I seem to be picking up her accent.

SALLY: You're acting in a play?

STEVE: Yep. Surprised the hell—pardon me—out of my-self. I was feeling like a fool to join this theatre, think-ing "What do I know about acting?"

SALLY: And now you're a leading man in more ways than one!

STEVE: Right on! They needed someone who looked like me—your sort of basic tall klutzy reporter type—and they didn't care about experience. I read for the part and got it right off. Then Lynne turned out to be the glamor-ous female lead. It didn't take long to go from romance on stage to romance in real life.

SALLY: Congratulations to you both. Thanks for calling back to tell me your good news.

STEVE: And thank you, Sally. You were really right about doing something different and getting out there, even if it did feel like being in a fishbowl at first.

I wish I could guarantee everybody who takes up a new interest Steve's results. I can't, but what I *can* guarantee is that every time you widen your horizons, you are benefit-ing *yourself* and making your life richer. You are growing internally. If you have a full life on your own hook, you don't *need* another person to make your life interesting, and you avoid that air of desperation that is such a turnoff to others. When you pursue your own interests, you are increasing your chances to meet others—and that special someone. Refusing to expand your life is the path to loneliness and isolation and long dreary evenings in front of the TV.

So get up and go out and do something! Get involved. Whatever you choose, it will be a step in the right direction.

PART FOUR

EXPECTATIONS AND REALITIES

13

Who's Your Fantasy?

I'VE ALREADY TALKED about the way the entertainment industry plays on our most unrealistic expectations—I call it the "MGM syndrome" (or MTV if you're younger). Here I'd like to explore in depth the role of fantasy in finding love.

Many of us have a movie running in our minds—some of us have only one, and it's always the same. Others are constantly rewriting their scripts. Usually it goes something like this: The hero is tall, dark, handsome and stalwart (that's you, or him). The heroine is sweet and blonde and perfect (that's you, or her). The story can be simple and direct or as complicated as a TV mini-series, complete with extra characters and extravagant settings. Either way, you are the main character, the producer, and the director. You're in charge. It's going to turn out *your* way no matter what. No one is walking off *this* set in a huff!

The stars are in perfect harmony—the music is soft, the lights are low (if it's a ski scene, the snow is perfect and the lodge romantic). This story never fails, it has the ending you want *because you are in control.*

The problem here is that no one can be in control of

another person. No matter how close your potential mate matches your personal fantasy, you aren't going to be able to control him/her.

Fantasy *can* serve a beneficial purpose—through it we can "try on" different people and situations in the privacy and safety of our own minds to see how we think they might work out. The trouble is that some of us get stuck in our own romantic scripts and deal ourselves out of the reality of a flesh-and-blood romance, with all its ups and downs and unpredictability.

If you stop to think about it a minute, you'll find that unpredictability is really a rather nice element in a romance—do you really want to know exactly how everything is going to turn out every time? It's that little edge of tension and suspense that gives love its zest.

But it's that old devil *flesh*—the kind real people come wrapped in—that causes all the trouble. Here you have very carefully designed Mr. or Ms. Perfect to your own exacting specifications—and here comes Mr. or Ms. Imperfect. What are you to do?

Well, sometimes these simplified fantasy types are easily overthrown by a nice hunk of reality—that blonde you've been carting about in your head turns out to be a luscious redhead—good-bye blondie! Or that tall, dark, lithe fellow has somehow slipped inside the rather portly skin of a charming, bearded Teddy-bear type who's only three inches taller than you. But love has bloomed, and hugability suddenly seems a lot more desirable than controllability.

Yet there are those of us who sink into our romantic fantasies so far that we can't *see* the forest for the trees. Insidiously, these little plays we write to fill up the void become the invisible standards against which we measure the people we meet and sometimes mate with. The prospective lover might be found wanting, not because of anything inherently inadequate in him or her, but because of a misfitting into the inner image machine.

Being unrealistic about who you want and why can be the reason you are alone.

So . . .

Let's talk about what you can *realistically* expect of a partner.

First, here's a list of ideas to help you be aware of your own personal fantasy. Check only those that apply to you, but be ruthlessly honest. Otherwise, you're wasting your time—self-defeating habits won't be weeded out.

- Someday my prince/princess will come and find me.
- The ideal person doesn't exist, so I'll have to settle for what I can get, which isn't much.
- My dream person is so wonderful that no one could possibly fill the bill.
- I spend a lot of time daydreaming about my lover-to-be.
- I meet a lot of people but no one comes close enough to my dream man/woman.
- No matter how nice a person seems, I'm always vaguely disappointed and dissatisfied by him/her.
- My ideal person is out there somewhere, all I have to do is keep looking.
- My ideal man/woman is very much like my father/ mother.
- It's vital that my parents approve my choice.
- My ideal person is the opposite of my same-sex parent.
- I want a marriage just like my parents'.
- I want a marriage nothing like my parents'.
- I know my mother/father would hate my ideal man/woman.
- Anyone who doesn't have at least 90 percent of my ideal's characteristics is going to fail me.
- My ideal lover has no face but a glorious body.
- It's hard for me to imagine an ideal person for myself.
- Every time I try somebody who isn't fairly like my dream person it's disaster.

- My "shopping list" for a mate includes exact physical characteristics, such as eye/hair color, height, weight/fitness level.
- My lover's occupation is a definite must on my list and it must be of equal or higher status.
- A person's education, family background, and social status largely influence my response to him/her.
- I expect a lover to instinctively know what pleases me.
- My fantasy man/woman would always want sex when I wanted it and be willing to please me.
- Getting the right lover will solve all my problems.
- I feel that if I don't find someone soon I'll have missed the romantic boat.
- The best part of life is being in love.
- I want someone primarily for sex.
- I'm looking for a partner who will/can share all of my interests and favorite activities.
- I want someone to exercise with.
- Romance for me means sharing everything.
- I want someone who is financially secure.
- I want my lover to be as much like me as possible.
- I do not want anyone who has other responsibilities, such as ex-wives, children, old parents.
- My ideal person is much younger/older than I am.
- Looks turn me on and I really want someone who looks like a model or a TV star.

If you checked more than five of the statements, take a closer look at what you're asking the universe to provide you with in a lover or mate. If you checked ten or more items, you may be operating on a level that is so unrealistic that no one will *ever* measure up. Nobody's perfect, and you don't have to eliminate your fantasy life entirely, but if it rules you and your choices about others, especially that one special other, you are probably either seeking control or approval in a relationship.

Your Reality Profile

Go back to Chapter Five, and review the "personality profile" you made up after you analyzed your personal style.

Now, still pretending that you are writing that ad for the personals columns, describe the person you want. Let yourself go. Be as detailed as you can. Think of everything you desire in your ideal lover/mate, including whatever fantasies come to your mind.

After you do that, take a good look at the two portraits you have drawn up—your own and your ideal lover's. See if they match. Would you expect to see these two people together? Is the person you've described too good to be true? Is he/she a carbon copy of the last person you had a relationship with, or maybe the total opposite? Are you bouncing from pillar to post?

Compare the description of the person you want today with past relationships—is there anything in common? Is what didn't work before a characteristic you are clinging to? For example, if you had a relationship in the past with an especially good-looking person and were then jealous of attention he/she got from others, have you revised your priorities into a more realistic mode or have you repeated this pattern in several romances?

Show your portraits to at least three close friends. Ask first if your own portrait comes close to how *they* see you. Then ask if your description of your desired opposite seems to fit who you are.

Take into consideration such mundane but eminently practical matters as where you live, what kind of job you have, what sorts of people you normally meet. Is it possible that you would be able to meet your wanted lover/mate in your ordinary life, or would you have to move to Hollywood or New York to find such a person?

After you've analyzed the reality quotient in your descriptions, go over them again. With your own in mind, make a list of all the qualities and/or characteristics that you *absolutely insist upon* in another person. (I would include such things as honesty, kindness, reliability, a sense of fun, and good grooming.) Second, make a list of those qualities you'd really like to have in another person but could, in a pinch, do without. Count this last batch, and figure that 10 or 15 percent is reasonable to expect of another (imperfect) human. Lastly, list all the things you'd *love* to have but which you know in your heart of hearts are *luxuries*. If you have a long list of these, you might be letting your interior movie rule your mind, and you might be missing *real* opportunities to find love.

The more you study these lists, the more you will become aware of just *who* your fantasy is, and how close reality can come to matching it.

Remember that the more strictures you put on who will be your love, the more you limit your opportunities of finding love.

No one can control another person, ever—and to think that you can is sheer folly. In order to get the kind of a relationship that can thrive, we have to give up this desire to be in control—not because it's wrong, but because it's unrealistic.

The only thing that we can reasonably expect to control is our own behavior and our response to the situations that life presents.

The search for approval is another that is doomed to failure. When you were a child, you looked to your parents for support and validation of yourself as an individual. What they gave you, whether it was total love and acceptance or coldness and disapproval, or some mixture thereof (known as mixed messages), affects you throughout life, and determines the extent to which you will seek—*or demand*—approval from your lovers.

If you're out there looking for first love, you need to evaluate whether what you are looking for is what you want or what you think your parents want for you—if it's an expression of your own deepest inner self or a need for approval and/or control.

If you've already had some relationships, you need to look for and identify the pattern you've been following, because even though each of your past mates may have seemed pretty unique at the time, there's *always* a pattern to past relationships, and it usually reflects what you needed and didn't get as a child. It's only by recognizing your own pattern that you can change it. It's been said that "you can't go home again," but I think that to be fully adult you must go home again—even if only in your mind. If the very idea of confronting your parents gives you the willies, they may be influencing you today in ways that need to be dealt with, and while I'm not a psychologist, I do think that a judicious dose of therapy—concentrating *just* on the problem at hand—can be very useful in stopping destructive patterns.

Unrealistic expectations take many forms. Can you believe that I once heard a woman say, quite sincerely horrified, of another woman's fiancé, "I could *never* marry a man who wore pink shirts!" Why not, pray tell? This particular man, who happened to have a fondness for pale pink shirts, was a prince of a guy—larky and funny, good to look at, charming, talented, successful. He was the kind of guy who saw the world through rose-colored glasses and always found the best in everything. I always thought those pink shirts were an expression of his view of life, and he always brought his girl pink roses by the armful. But this woman saw pink shirts as unmanly, and nothing was ever going to change her opinion. I often wanted to ask her if she'd prefer a man who wore black shirts . . . but of course I never did. What pink shirts represented to her I never found out.

Men, particularly, are prone to "their type." Whether it's the Dolly Parton type—the buxom blonde—or the

Cher type—the tall, lean brunette, often their women run true to type. Why?

When men get together, after the first couple of beers or drinks, their conversation most always turns to the "type" of woman they prefer. One will gaze into the far distance and claim his susceptibility to the "ice princess." Another will confess his vulnerability to red hair and freckles, or the blonde with dark eyes, or the "true" brunette . . .

A lot of men *breeze* through their younger years firmly attached to this typing. Whether it derived from an early acquaintance with *Playboy* magazine or from the influence of first love, it usually represents a fairly standardized idea of what is—or what is supposed to be—appealing in the female. Men who keep pursuing specific colorations or body configurations simply need to become more attuned to their *own* inner needs and desires. Physical features are like wrappings—and every package must be unwrapped before you can find out what's inside, right?

If you have strong responses that aren't quite rational, I suggest you give it some thought or perhaps seek counseling. It might have nothing to do with the present, real you. In fact, more than anything it often indicates a lack of self-esteem. When you really know and have accepted who you are (and changed all you could reasonably expect to change), you will no longer have this need to control or seek approval. *Then* you can relax and be open to appreciate someone else—*without* becoming sidetracked by their outer trappings.

Speaking of professional help, I'd like to talk for a bit here about what is becoming apparent as a major problem in the lives of many people; parental stereotypes and the unconscious recreating of the past in adult relationships. People who suffer from these problems may have had extraordinarily difficult childhoods, or been abused— physically, sexually, and/or emotionally—as children.

As child abuse is coming more and more out into the open, more and more people are allowing themselves to admit to their own abused childhoods. These conditions leave deep scars in the psyche. And these scars can affect adult relationships, often causing the abused child to become an abusing parent, or causing a man who saw his father abuse his mother to become a wife-batterer himself.

If you have any of this type of misfortune in your own background, please do seek professional counseling. You need the support of someone who understands and can offer the right empathetic help.

Many people also are the product of families in which one or both parents were alcoholics, and this kind of background results in many problems for these adult children of alcoholics. There are now national organizations for people with these types of backgrounds. They are easy to find. Alcoholics Anonymous, which has chapters in cities large and small, is a good source of information. Another organization is called Adult Children of Alcoholics and would be listed in your phone book, or your local AA chapter could refer you to a local group. These meetings are free and they are extremely helpful support groups for people suffering the residual problems of these troubled backgrounds.

Again, the whole point is to be *aware*. However you do it—whether you get to that point by reading this book and taking the quizzes, or with some professional help—you've got to do it. It's as simple as that. There's no shortcut to self-knowledge.

And then it'll be infinitely easier to recognize what someone *else* is all about. And an intrinsic part of that recognition is your acceptance of how fallible we *all* are. Love, to be good, recognizes that fantasy is nice but reality is better—and that humans come in all shapes and sizes, with varying talents and accomplishments, each one unique, just as *you* are unique.

Now, suppose you've found love and—*ouch!*—it didn't work. Let's go on to talk about *that*.

14

How to Cope with Rejection

BEFORE YOU ARE completely equipped to look for love, you need to know how to handle rejection. Everyone gets rejected at some time or other. The last incidence of boy-meets-girl-marries-and-lives-happily-ever-afterhappened in a movie in 1948.

Nothing lasts forever—not life, not love. So let's talk about what to do if rejection hits.

Whether we want to or not, most of us do paint a rosier picture of our past loves than the truth would allow. For example, my friend Gloria suffered a bad breakup with Grant. She was crying a lot. I asked her what she missed most.

"Those walks through the park," she said, bursting into fresh tears (the sun happened to be shining at the time and it was a park-walking day). "I *loved* those walks we used to take."

Every day? Well, no, not *every* day. Only on weekends then? No, not weekends either. When?

With a little examination Gloria realized that in a whole year with Grant they had taken exactly three walks through the park! Her tears began to dry. She was learning perspective.

In this chapter we're going to discuss specific techniques for dealing with rejection. One of these is a "Love Journal," a trick I learned a long time ago. Keeping a record of a relationship on a day-to-day basis is the best way to insure that you'll have a balanced picture of the affair if it ends.

Let's return to Gloria. When she met Chris and fell in love again, Gloria was careful to keep a Love Journal, recording the daily ups and downs of the relationship. When the affair with Chris ended she went back to her journal and counted the times she had blown up (or wanted to blow up) at him for forgetting appointments with her and for his sloppinesss around the house. Furthermore, Gloria's journal showed that she was indeed repeating a pattern. Even though Grant and Chris at first blush seemed to be as different as day and night, careful study revealed that *she* was putting pressure on the relationship. She was self-destructing. She suddenly realized that while she might now be alone, she wasn't standing in the rain with theater tickets at 9:00 P.M. or picking up somebody else's dirty socks, underwear, and towels.

Rejection comes in all sizes and shapes, and it afflicts all ages. The following call is an all-too-typical example of how the *fear* of rejection operates, even in the very young.

MEG: Hi, Sally. Can I ask you a question?

SALLY: Sure. Shoot.

MEG: It's about getting rejected.

SALLY: What about getting rejected?

MEG: Well, I've got this boyfriend and my friends are all telling me that he's going to reject me and I'm scared of getting hurt.

SALLY: How old are you, Meg?

MEG: Fourteen.

SALLY: Is this your first romantic relationship?

MEG: Yes, it is.

SALLY: Let me tell you something. Don't you listen to your friends. Just go ahead and love to the best of your ability. That's what's important.

MEG: But what if he does reject me, like they say?

SALLY: If that happens, then you chalk that up on a little board as Rejection Number One. Because by the time you're ready to settle down with your one and only, you will have rejected two or three men yourself, and you will have been rejected by two or three. *If* you're living right. Until that happens, you're not experienced, and until you're experienced, you're not ready to really love.

MEG: You mean that my boyfriend might reject me and that then it might even happen two more times before I find the right man?

SALLY: Yep. That's exactly what I mean. So you just go ahead and love and live. And if this boyfriend does reject you, remember you have two more to go!

MEG: Thanks, Sally. So long.

My philosophy is that *everybody* in circulation should have at least three loves at the same time. One on the fire, two waiting in the wings. The point is, don't carry all your eggs in one basket. Then, if one gets broken, you'll still have five more. And, if four more get broken, you'll still have at least one. This is a common, oft-repeated mistake that a lot of people make. They meet a "person of the opposite sex," and immediately begin to hang all their hopes for a happy, passionate, and rosy future on that person. Take my advice: *don't*. If you've had thirty-three, you're probably a "love junkie." But if you are stuck with the idea that you are only supposed to have one "great" love, you're being unrealistic. Termination is a fact of life. How you handle it is what makes the difference between misery and recovery.

Why? To get a bit philosophical for a minute, I have a theory that each person comes into your life for a specific reason, to teach you a lesson that you need to know, and to learn a lesson for him/herself.

But when rejection hits, you may not be in a position to be or feel very philosophical. (That will come later.) So first, you have to be practical. What I'm going to do is give you a ten-step plan for coping with rejection and healing your emotions and your psyche as quickly as possible—but not *too* quickly. The healing process is part of the learning process. The pain of the rejection is there to teach you something, and if you don't learn it the first (or second or third) time around, you're going to have to keep going through it until you do learn.

And the best way to learn it is to give yourself *time*. One of the big questions I'm frequently asked is *How long does it take to recover from a break-up?* Curiously, men seem to be more concerned about this issue than women, as was Ken, who called me after his seven-year marriage broke up.

KEN: Hi, Sally. I'm really glad to talk to you. I'm hurtin' bad.

SALLY: Sorry to hear that. What's the problem?

KEN: My wife left me.

SALLY: Ouch! You've got a right to be hurting.

KEN: (Sadly) I know. I haven't got anything left. She got the kids and the house and I'm here in a motel room by myself until I can find a decent place to live. There's not even a TV—but I'm glad, because that's how I found you, listening to the radio.

SALLY: Welcome to radioland! How can I help you?

KEN: Sally, I'm forty-two. I didn't get married too early—I was thirty-five and too busy with my career when I was younger, so I don't have much experience with this kind of thing. Can you tell me how long I'm going to suffer? I mean, I can cope with it if I only know how long I'm going to feel this way.

SALLY: That's a good attitude. How long were you married?

KEN: Seven years. Two kids.

SALLY: Okay. And how long has it been since she left you?

KEN: It was just a couple of weeks ago. She said she wanted to be alone to find herself.

SALLY: So you don't think there's any hope of a reconciliation?

KEN: No. She told me she doesn't love me anymore either. I just want to get over this awful feeling that things will never be right again and get on with my work and my life. But I can't see any end to this pain.

SALLY: Don't worry. There is an end. It's not going to be easy, it never is. But in a couple of years you'll be a new man.

KEN: (Incredulously) Two years? I don't think I could stand this for that long.

SALLY: Think about what you were doing for the past two years.

KEN: Well—gee, I can hardly remember. It went so fast.

SALLY: So will the next two years. What happens when there's a break-up of a long-term relationship, psychologically, is that the first few weeks are intensely painful. Then, depending on how long the relationship lasted, there's a period of time when the abandoned person feels grief and goes around in a state of shock, slightly dazed all the time, feeling he (or she) has been in a major battle. The whole process of healing takes about a third of the time that the relationship lasted. In your case, that's a total of about two years, maybe a bit more.

KEN: And then it'll be over?

SALLY: No. After about six months, you'll move through the next phase to complete the utter recovery. That's why it's important *not* to enter into another relationship at this point. All of you out there listening, hear this in your ears. It's vital you go through the entire grief and mourning and healing process before you get involved again. Otherwise, you'll always be a member of the "walking wounded."

KEN: What if it doesn't go away in a few years?

SALLY: Then you're holding onto the pain, for whatever reason. Sometimes the pain gets to feel comfortable just because it's familiar, and then we don't let it go. Like putting your tongue into a sore tooth, just to make sure it still hurts. It's begun to feel good to you.

KEN: So I have to make an effort to let the pain go?

SALLY: That's it. Go through it, feel it, and then let it go.

KEN: Thanks, Sally. You've really helped me tonight.

SALLY: Okay. Hang in there. You'll recover.

The next lesson you need to be aware of is—*don't put all your eggs in somebody else's basket*. If you are operating under the assumption that the main thing in life is to be somebody else's love, you're inviting failure and rejection. That's a heavy trip to lay on another body. As we've said in earlier chapters, the more you have going for yourself—awareness, interests, friends, activities—the less you're going to fall apart when a relationship ends.

Okay, so everybody makes mistakes and even the best-laid eggs do sometimes get broken. What to do about it?

There are five distinct phases to the rejection process and what needs to follow it for healing and recuperation. For each of these, we've divided the process into two stages, and these two-part, five-phase segments make up our ten-step plan to complete recovery.

The five phases through which we must go in order to successively cope with rejection and make a complete recovery are much the same as those involved with loss by death, for the loss of a loved one *for any reason* is a severe drain on our emotional resources. They are:

1. Angst
2. Anger
3. Analysis
4. Acceptance
5. Action

Compare these five stages to the fingers of your hand. Each has a separate function, but together they operate as a unit. And just as you'd find your normal daily activities impaired if you burned your thumb or cut your pinky, you'll have to suffer through the emotional disruption of your daily life as you go through all these phases, consecutively and completely, before you'll be able to return to your normally functioning self.

Angst is the German word for pain, and it has come to mean that mental anguish we call despair. It is the first, and in some ways most important, step of the healing process.

Oddly enough, many people do not allow themselves to feel grief—not even when a loved one dies. For some reason, this cleansing and healing emotion is denied. And when it is denied, it festers, just like an improperly cleaned wound would. Feeling the pain is important.

So, *Step One* is *allow yourself to feel the pain*. You've been hurt. Take it seriously. As seriously as you would a broken leg or a malfunctioning kidney. No, you can't go to a doctor and get your broken heart set in a plaster cast, or get a pill for that leaky valve that seems to be your tear ducts these days, but you can encourage yourself to let go and feel the hurt.

Step Two is *wallow in it*. That's right, get right into that pain and depression and feelings of hate and frustration. Don't for one minute feel guilty about all those hateful things you are thinking about that rotten person who hurt you so much. Go all the way. Feel sorry for yourself. Do whatever you feel like doing, even if it's really off the wall.

Revert to childhood, eat too much, drink too much, don't take off your pajamas all day, let the dishes go, don't shave or bathe—whatever makes you feel comfortably and happily *miserable*. Tell a couple of good friends what you're going through and get their permission to call them whenever you want to cry or complain.

Just don't carry this part of the process too far. Set a

limit, a day or a week or even a bit longer if you are really in bad shape. But do plan a cut-off point. Take off a couple of days from work if necessary—or use a weekend. Turn off the phone. Vegetate. Stay in bed.

After you've done this, you'll be glad to have a hot bath and a good meal. Junk food will have lost its appeal. Remember not to feel a bit guilty about anything during this period. Then you're ready for *anger*.

Part One of the anger phase is to think negative.

SALLY'S BASIC RULE

Forget all you've heard to the contrary and remember all the rotten things you can about him/her. Dwell on it. Call the offending person all the bad names you can think of. Think how glad you now are you don't have to put up with that anymore. Remember the fights and the bad times. Make a "hit" list of all the disappointments and broken dates, everything rotten he/she ever did or said and look at it every time you begin to feel nostalgic.

Part Two of *anger* is to let go on yourself. Go ahead, go over all the dumb things *you* did to contribute to the breakup. Call yourself all the bad names you want to. Be as hard as you possibly can on your poor hurting self. The idea is to make yourself so darned miserable that you'll be *glad* to feel good again.

Once you've done this, you're ready for *analysis*. Here's where you start to use your head instead of your heart.

First, using some of the techniques you've learned in this book, take an honest look at the relationship. Were you really ready—was he/she really ready? Were you operating from need—the neurotic kind that hooks people up together not because they're truly in love but because they are getting some "payoff" out of the relationship?

Do you feel helpless and bereft without the other person now? Is this because you really can't manage or just because you are choosing not to do so? Is your self-image damaged?

Part two of the *analysis* phase is to see what you can do to make sure you don't make the same mistake again. Look for patterns—is this a repeat number of the last man/woman you were involved with again? Does this "always happen" to you? Was there some genuine incompatibility that just couldn't be helped? Did Fate intervene in some way you couldn't help?

Next comes *acceptance*.

That's right. You have to accept that that other person and you aren't going together any more and aren't going to get back together.

Part One of this phase is to make sure that you are clear of the emotional remains. If you're going to hang in there, hoping he/she will come back to you, it's no good. This requires a ruthless weeding-out of those old memories.

Part Two of *acceptance* is to make manifest your determination to heal and go on with your own life. In this part of the process you throw out all those records that were "your" songs. You stop sleeping in his old shirt, or you put that photo album of the vacation you took her on in the attic with your high school graduation album. It's part of the past now. Treat it that way. Stop looking for reasons why . . .

Acceptance is followed by *action!*

That's why you're reading this book. Action means getting out there and, armed with new knowledge (by that I mean self-knowledge), getting back into the romantic fray. You know what they say: get back on the horse that threw you.

The first step in this direction is to go back and make

sure you're ready. You may not be ready for quite a long time. It may take weeks or even months for the wound to heal. That's okay. There are lots of other kinds of action you can take while you're completing the healing process.

Take up a new interest—a sport, a hobby, some volunteer work. Open up your eyes to the world. Even a cursory look will show you that there are lots of people out there worse off than you are. And any new skill or activity will help repair your battered self-esteem.

Part Two of the *action* phase is to get out there and seek a new love. You may want to refurbish your wardrobe, get a new hairdo, even move to a new town. In this last phase of the process, you must consider yourself first.

Take care of your health, your appearance, do your apartment or house over, go on a wild and wonderful vacation. Break out in some way. Spend all your spare cash on something extravagant you've always wanted. Go to the movies every day for a week. Give a party and ask all your friends to bring one stranger you haven't met. Buy flowers for yourself, pretend it's your birthday.

By putting yourself in an up mood, you'll be sending out the vibes to attract someone new. Moping around will only keep you paralyzed. Work on yourself—make a list of all the good things about you. List your accomplishments over the last five years. Ask three friends each to tell you three qualities of yours that they admire.

Think of all the wonderful possibilities life has to offer. Love is only one of them.

15

How to Get Rid of Somebody

THE OTHER SIDE of the coin of rejection is when *you* have to do the rejecting. This can be just as painful as being on the receiving end. Most of us don't enjoy hurting another, even when we know it's the right thing to do.

What's the best way to tell someone that you're through?

Cutting down on the emotional damage for *both* of you is essential, and there are techniques for doing this.

This is probably one of the hardest things any of us ever has to face. But one of the things about being the one who leaves instead of the one who is left is that you come to understand that all of those hurtful things—the broken promises, the telephone calls that weren't, the excuses, the forgetfulness—aren't really meant to wound. They are usually kind attempts to let the other one down easily. And they never work. If you've been on the receiving end, you know.

Listen to the story of Mary Lou and Joe.

Tonight was going to be important, and Mary Lou was a nervous wreck. She was fixing a special dinner for Joe. Not to celebrate anything—to tell him she was through. For weeks she'd known that she and Joe just weren't right for each other. Not only did they have sex problems, but every time Mary Lou tried to talk about them Joe froze up, denying they existed. So, she had made up her mind to end it.

She knew it wasn't going to be easy. Joe had a mean temper, especially after a few drinks. And he could be foul-mouthed when upset. Usually it wasn't directed at her, but she'd seen it plenty of times in the past.

After consulting with her girl friend Marsha and her cousin Billy, both of whom knew Joe well, she planned a quiet, intimate dinner for the two of them during which, she thought, they'd be able to talk sensibly. She decided to cook Joe's favorite dishes, have candles and a good wine. She thought the nice atmosphere would soften the blow. As she shopped, she reasoned that Joe would be put in a good mood to receive the bad news. She rehearsed her "breakup speech," envisioning herself coolly and rationally telling him that they had to part.

The night came. She took special care over the supper. He arrived with flowers, an uncharacteristic gesture that took her off guard. He commented happily how good the lasagna smelled. She smiled in welcome, but when he tried to kiss her she pulled away.

"Hey, what's wrong? Do I have bad breath or something?" he said, hurt and on the edge of anger.

"It's nothing. I've just got to go and finish the sauce and make the salad. I had to work late. Why don't you fix a drink while you're waiting?"

Unsettled, Mary Lou had a hard time getting things straight in the kitchen, and Joe polished off three quick Scotches while she was getting the food on the table. Nonetheless, she opened the wine and poured it.

The dinner progressed through the lasagna and the bottle of wine to coffee and after-dinner drinks on the living room couch. Joe was feeling heady and amorous. As she fended him off, panic-stricken, she launched into her prepared speech about their incompatibility. Joe, more than a bit tipsy and feeling the need for sex, lashed out at this unexpected rejection.

"What the hell are you talking about, babe? Of course we're good for each other! Come on over here and let me show you just how good for you I am."

In spite of her unpleasant resolve, Mary Lou—to avoid the scene she saw coming and its unpleasant aftermath—went into his arms and into bed. In the morning, after yet another night of bad sex, she knew more than ever she had to break up with Joe. Only now she had to start from scratch.

What did Mary Lou do wrong? Her intentions were the best. She took well-meaning advice. But what she hadn't considered—or didn't know—is that the *only* place to break up with someone, *especially* someone volatile like Joe, is in a public place.

An awful lot of people care. They reach the point where they *love* the other person, as you'd love a friend, but they *know* that they're not *in love* with the person. Then they realize, sadly, that they have to break up. And if that sounds familiar, I guess it's because it's happened to nearly everybody on earth.

You're very comfortable with the person, you've had a tremendous intimacy. How can you hurt this person? You might say to me, "Sally, this is different. I love my friends. I love my family. This is even closer and more intimate." That may well be true, but, if it isn't the top shot, you have to go on further. And this is the hardest thing to do. It's quite easy to drop a casual friend, or to ignore someone who annoys you, or to stomp off from someone who's hurt you beyond all endurance. But when it gets to the point where the person is second on the rung, too much to be an ordinary friend but not quite the person you want to make that long-term commitment to, how do you say good-bye?

Here is my ten-step plan to minimize the emotional damage to both the person you're breaking up with and yourself.

1. *Make sure you are completely ready to break up.*
    If you have any doubts about whether you are ready to make the final break—*don't*. First, think about it carefully. All through this book we've been advising you to think—to analyze. True, you may have "gut" feelings you can trust, and if you do you won't be having any trouble knowing this is it. But if you're like most of us, you'll look at the good along with the bad and have some vacillation going on there. If you're seesawing back and forth, make a list. Writing down what you're feeling is the best way to clarify your feelings. And whatever you do, do it in a cool mood—not in a burst of "I'm finally fed up with you" anger. A written record will also give you something to go back to for reinforcement afterward.
2. *Don't think ever that you are going to keep him/her as a friend. Trying to maintain a "friendship" with an ex-lover/spouse is just another way of hanging on to the relationship. It can't be done, and if you try, you're kidding yourself.*
    One of the biggest mistakes people make when they are breaking up is to think that they are going to—somehow—process the relationship onto some other plane, where the two of you share a whole lot of wonderful stuff together because you've shared it before (especially if there's no great pain involved over the course of the relationship that's ending). You imagine that you can continue this while you go off and date others so you can find Mr./Ms. Right, and this person will then be your second-level good friend and confidant. Well, it sounds good, but it won't work. Why? Because there is no way of keeping that level

of friendship operating if one of you is over the line and is in love. If somebody is in love with you, you have to be sensitive enough to know that. You have to realize that you owe them something. And here's what you owe them: you owe them being as delicate and as sensitive as possible. Handling this moment sensitively will help you avoid the "guilties" later.

So if he/she suggests that you see one another once in a while, have dinner, go to a movie, say a firm *no*. Be as gentle and kind as you can. Say "I'm sorry, but it just won't work to keep on seeing each other under any circumstances. I need a clean slate at least for awhile."

Once you've made up your mind, make no contact and accept no contact. Don't hang out where you know or even suspect you'll run into him/her. Don't call to say "how are you?" (The answer will be "awful.") If he/she calls you, be polite, but detached and distant. Say you really can't talk because you have someone over. Ask him/her please not to call for a few months because it won't do any good. And don't keep in touch through mutual friends.

One man I knew hung out at his ex-mother-in-law's for weeks after the divorce, just to keep tabs on his ex-wife and make sure she was okay. This sort of thing only exacerbates the disturbance to all involved. Mutual friends have their own problems when a couple breaks up. Do them the favor of excluding them from your ex-relationship.

3. *Be brave—explain*.

The coward never really explains what's going on. The extreme form of this is the person who just disappears, leaving a huge unexplained gap in the other person's life. The most negative reason for leaving another person is much more comforting to him/her than no reason at all. Two women I knew some

years ago who happened to be roommates both lost
their loves at almost the same time. Linda's boyfriend
did all the usual sidestepping little acts until finally
she confronted him with a frank, "What's wrong?"
His answer was "I'm sorry but I just don't love you
anymore." Sure, it hurt, but at least she *knew*, and
more important, she knew there wasn't anything she
could do about it. Within a couple of months, she was
dating again and much happier than before, because
there was no ambiguity. The other woman, Sandra,
was in love with a man who did a complete vanishing
act. One day he just upped and disappeared. He
wouldn't answer her letters pleading for an explanation. A full year later she was plotting to run into him
through a mutual friend, still unhappily nagging a
what-on-earth-could-it-have-been-we-were-so-happy.
If her lover had been sensitive, he would have told her
the reason for his decision, thereby helping her to heal
sooner. There's *nothing* more corroding to a person's
self-esteem than being refused the opportuniy to know
something definite. It can bother them *years* later.
Was it bad breath? Bad sex? Did he/she offend in
some unknown way? Was the lover swept away by a
rival? Cowardice is *immoral,* and the archcoward, like
Sandra's man, is *cruel.* One night she was beloved,
the most wonderful girl in the world, and the next she
had apparently ceased to exist! I suspect that the
archcoward suffers pangs of guilt for such dastardly
behavior—nobody likes *knowing* that he/she is a
coward. So don't be—for your own sake as well as
for the sake of the person you're leaving.

4. *Have a heart-to-heart talk in person.*
    In person is the key here. Don't *ever* do it with a
    telephone call. Too impersonal. And a letter is even
    worse. Plan your strategy. Pick your time. And then
    sit down with the person, preferably in a public place,

like a quiet, intimate restaurant (but *not* one of your favorite haunts as a couple—keep it neutral). Then, if things get out of hand, there are less likely to be any ugly scenes. Never criticize or blame the other person. Don't say that he/she wasn't this or that to you. Simply indicate that you have other needs. You're in a position to be magnanimous: blame yourself.

5. *Consider timing.*

Don't, for example, break up a long-running (or even a short) relationship just before a major holiday. This will leave the person feeling even *more* abandoned and isolated. Choose a time that is as neutral as you can manage, even if it means waiting a few days or a few weeks. This waiting period, if it is necessary, will also give *you* the chance to cool down and handle it with a minimum of explosive emotion. If your lover is going through any sort of crisis, wait. Be supportive, as you would to any friend. And do yourself the same favor. If you are going through a trauma, or a major change (job, family, health), don't add insult to injury—wait until things simmer down.

Picking a fight to bring things to a head or tearing the other person down is lower than low. Pour on the healing oil of praise. Tell the other person that he/she is wonderful and attractive, fascinating and delightful, but that right now you need something different. Be honest. *If you've found someone else, say so,* without going into details. If you're just wanting out, admit that you want to be free to look for someone who more closely meets your needs. Everybody has needs. You're entitled. Say it has nothing to do with him/her, no faults, no deficiencies, just you and your needs. Allow a *long* evening—at least a two-hour dinner—to accomplish this.

6. *Don't try to taper off.*

Let's say you've been in a relationship for a while and you've done it right. You've become friends and lovers, but you're just not ready for a total commitment. It could be for any reason—maybe you're not ready, maybe you had one too soon before, or maybe you've met someone else who really seems to be Mr./Ms. Right. Whatever the reason, don't drag out the relationship you're planning to cut off. One of the peculiarities of human nature is that once one party knows the other one wants out, he/she instantly becomes much more in love. The incipient break-up, like the domestic row, is also fertile ground for a renewal of romance in the relationship. To keep or get him/her back, you go on best behavior, trying often to re-create your early, halcyon days together. Don't let this happen. Don't allow yourself to be rewooed in any shape, form, or style.

7. *Make sure your message gets across.*

Give hints and clues as a preliminary to the final delivery of the blow. For at least a week before you make it terminal, show the person in little ways that you are dissatisfied. Bring up the things that have been bothering you, and try to talk them over. Don't let it be a bolt from the blue. This warning time need not be very long—a month at most, depending on other factors, and a week as a minimum—for the person to get a bit used to the idea. Chances are he/she already knows things aren't what they used to be, or as they should be, but has been avoiding admitting this. Or perhaps both of you have been skirting the problem. And if you get some talking started, it will give you the opportunity to use cool logic instead of hot emotion. You can't tiptoe out of a relationship—there has to be a final confrontation. Prepare the ground so that it will take.

8. *Don't let yourself get caught with someone else.*
Whatever you do, don't stoop to this rotten trick. It's much worse than the archcoward's total disappearing act and much more painful. It's demeaning to *everybody* involved (you'll feel terrible about it afterward). So, if you *have* found a new love, don't start until the old one is properly laid to rest. And if even the tiniest chance of your getting caught in any kind of an intimate situation with another person exists, stamp it out ruthlessly and at once. It's mean and cruel, tawdry and beneath you, ugly and cheap, low, unthinking, uncaring, and selfish. You owe the other person better treatment than that. Not to mention the guilt trip you'll be laying on yourself! That pain of finding someone you love with someone else is just too horrible to describe. It's the absolute *worst* way to end a relationship. No one deserves this humiliation.

9. *Be prepared for his/her reaction.*
This announcement is bound to cause pain. Like any other profound loss, it should be handled with dignity and genuine caring. The person may cry (even if he's a man) or go into a monumental slump and not want to talk or react at all. You may have to see him/her home. He/she may call you up in the middle of the night, needing comfort. Stand for it. You owe it to him/her to be there for support, for talking, explaining, tears, whatever for at least a period of time, a week at the most. You don't owe him/her one last night of lovemaking and you don't owe it to him/her to let it drag on. After a week, cut it off. If the need persists beyond a week, then you must say another, firmer, good-bye. Tell him/her it's *over*. *Kaput. Finished.* Wish him/her the best, then withdraw. Completely. Ultimately, it is the kindest thing you can do because it helps him/her accept reality.

10. *Don't look back.*

Anybody who's been rejected is likely to punch all your buttons to try to get you back. But you are in charge. If you've handled the breakup as sensitively as I've advised, then you'll be able to resist any attempts to make you feel guilty. Cutting the cord, eliminating contact, making sure you don't go where you're likely to be seen are absolutely necessary. Leave a cold trail behind you. Don't steal his/her friends and tell your friends not to mention you to him/her, even if asked. Going back after you've broken up can result in agonizing ambiguity. Giving a doomed relationship another shot is futile. You can't unscramble an egg. Trying again after you've decided it's over will only mean that you will have to go through the whole messy painful process again, diminishing your chances of a peaceful and healing resolution. Don't do it.

16

Dating

A FIRST DATE has the power to reduce even the most
mature of us to the status of teenagers—especially the
newly-single, who may not have dated since youth. Why?
Because every first date is an encounter with the person
who may be your permanent mate.

A dozen questions arise at once: no matter who is doing
the asking (or how), there's always that little edge of fear
or, at least, anxiety. What to do? How to say it? What to
expect? What if it doesn't work out?

We've made a simple plan to guide you over the dangerous shoals of the first date. Like everything else in this
book, the way to ease is thorough planning.

Usually it's the unplanned, so-called *spontaneous* date
that gets people into a state of acute discomfort. Not
knowing what to expect, both parties often flounder. The
knowledge that this *might* be the beginning of a budding
romance creates anxiety.

So what's so troublesome about the first date? Well, the
very fact that it is *first*.

Take the example of Susan whose phone has just rung
on a Friday evening. A man she met at a party last week is

calling. "Hi, this is Jim. We met at Jane's party last week."

"Hi!" she responds. "How are you?"

"Fine, thanks. What about you?"

After a bit of this initial roundabout, Jim says,

"Are you free on Saturday?"

At this point, she doesn't know what to answer. Saturday *when?* If she has no Saturday night date, she might not want to admit this to a relative stranger. On the other hand, she might like to go out Saturday. But he hasn't given her even a hint of his plan, if he has one. Suppose she says she's free.

"Great! How about lunch then?"

That leaves her accepting in advance, even though Saturday lunch is not what she might prefer to do. Now it's too late to make an excuse, or at best awkward to respond by saying that, "Gee, I thought you meant Saturday night."

That statement would only make her look a bit desperate.

If she says she's not free, she risks losing the date entirely.

This relationship is already off to a bad start, and the crucial first date hasn't even happened yet!

SALLY'S BASIC RULE

Be specific. Have a plan before you call and tell the person exactly what you have in mind.

For example, if Jim had said immediately that he'd like to invite Susan to lunch on Saturday, she could either decline or accept, according to her mood and schedule. She is not in the position of saying she "has nothing on" for Saturday night, but is in a position to suggest an alternate Saturday afternoon idea. If lunch isn't ideal, or she's shy about sharing a meal on a first date, she can say she's busy for lunch but free afterward and suggest meeting for coffee or a walk in the park. This tells Jim that the date will be relatively cost-free, even though as the inviter he is assuming responsibility to pay.

Not all first dates need to be one-on-one. Younger people seem not to date in the traditional manner at all, and double dates and group dates are just fine for them. Hanging out, however, doesn't signify much interest. To ask another person to hang out isn't as effective as having a specific plan, even for a group date. Saying that so-and-so is having a few people over in the afternoon or evening and inviting the date to come along is much better.

There are all sorts of activities available to the person who is somewhat shy and doesn't feel up to doing a lot of talking. Some alternatives are antique shows, flea markets, church bazaars, street fairs, community affairs, or animal shows.

These have the advantage of a low admission price, and they provide automatic topics of conversation as well as a degree of busy-ness and neutrality that help to cover the almost inevitable awkward moments of silence. One can always point at something different to see and be commented upon. Also, they are neutral. A movie requires some degree of mutuality and discussion of likes and dislikes, and an initial disagreement may mean starting off on the wrong foot, although some lovers never enjoy the same movies and end up going alone or with a friend.

I'm often asked about women asking men out. This seems to be one of the big concerns about dating. Is it okay for a woman to ask a man out? Emphatically, YES. The men I've talked to—including my male TV audiences on a show I did on just this topic—assure me that they are very flattered and receptive to being asked out by a woman.

Of course, there may be men who still want that old male prerogative, but you'll never know until you try.

Take the story of Robin, a twenty-three-year old who was called up for jury duty. Since her job didn't pay her if she didn't work, she wasn't thrilled to do her civic duty, but went anyway. As the trial progressed, she was very impressed by the young assistant D.A. who was prosecuting the case. He was competent . . . and he was handsome. After the trial was over, one of the other jurors, an older woman, commented on what a handsome man the A.D.A. was, and Robin sighed, "Yeah!"

"Why don't you call him up" asked the woman.

"Me? How could I do that? I don't even know him. I don't even know his name."

"His name's posted, silly," she replied, supplying the name.

"But how would I get in touch with him?"

"Call the D.A.'s office and ask for him. Just leave a message with your name and office phone number."

Robin really wanted to call the handsome A.D.A., but she'd never done *anything* like that in her life. She asked me what to do. I said, "Call him. What do you have to lose?"

Later, she told me she had sweaty palms, but she managed to screw up her courage and it turned out to be a breeze. The D.A.'s office took the message and he called her back the next afternoon. On the edge of fainting from anxiety, she told him who she was, that she was "the short blond girl" in the jury of the case he'd tried on Wednesday. As she's quite pretty, he'd noticed her too, and he was pleased as punch that she'd had the gumption to seek him out. At least she knew his name, while he didn't know hers!

There followed a date and a few more dates. It fizzled after a coule of months, but they had fun while it lasted. When I asked Robin if she was sorry she'd taken the chance, she said a resounding NO. She'd do it again. What it did was to bolster her self-confidence, show her that she didn't have to stand in wings waiting for a man to call her, and gave her a sense of having greater control over her romantic life. Now, she's not reticent at all about asking out a man she finds appealing.

So let me encourage my women readers to go and do likewise, following the general list of *do's* and *don'ts* that follows. They apply no matter which sex is doing the asking out.

Here are some points to remember for first-date etiquette:

DO

- Plan for a time you're likely to be in a good mood. A date isn't a cure for depression.
- Be enthusiastic—but not hyper.
- Have a definite plan, and an alternate plan. It's the best way to be relaxed.
- Stay reasonably near where you live, if possible, so that you'll be able to get home easily.
- Meet someplace neutral. A man may prefer to call for a woman at her home or apartment, but if a woman does the inviting, it's okay to suggest meeting somewhere.
- Hone your conversation skills. Have something to say. Read a newspaper or news magazine, have opinions to discuss.
- Be clear about where you are going and what sort of dress is appropriate. If, for example, you are inviting someone to a party given by a friend of yours, be sure to say "dress casually," or "people will be dressing up." If it's a restaurant, mention the type and give a clue about what to wear. Say, "It's Italian, with checkered tablecloths and candles in wine bottles—nothing fancy," or "René's is a nice French restaurant—sort of medium dressy."

- Have alternate suggestions prepared. If you receive a "No!" to your question "Do you like Chinese food?" don't let that be the only apple in your barrel.
- Indicate sincerely to the other person that your main objective is the pleasure of his/her company. If you're "on the make" or just asking the person out because you're at loose ends, it'll show.
- The same applies for accepting a date. Accept only if you are genuinely interested in getting to know the other person.
- Telephone for the specific purpose of asking for the date.
- Always have a specific day and time of day, as well as an activity to offer. "Would you like to go to a piano recital on Sunday afternoon at three and then have coffee and cake afterward?" *Never say* "Are you free . . . ?" or be vague about plans.
- Be sure to mention if food is to be part of the occasion, and say what type and when, as above. If it's a party, say it will include drinks and snacks, or say specifically that it is a buffet, outdoor barbeque, or sit-down dinner.
- Advise the person if there is anything unusual about the circumstances—such as an outdoor concert that might require bringing a blanket, or a sailing date that requires boat shoes and a waterproof jacket.
- Choose the daylight hours for a first date.
- Select a lunch date if you're in the same business.
- Have an escape route planned if you're bored. Be organized so you can say you have another appointment later and do it gracefully.
- Know your neighborhood—what's going on, events of interest, pleasant hangouts, etc.
- Read the social columns to keep up with events in your town, and check the Arts and Leisure section from your newspaper.
- Know what *you* like to do so you don't have to go fishing for suggestions from the other person.

- Remember that the first date is like going to a casino— use your instincts and get your timing right.
- If you're a woman, *ask men out*. They love it!
- Pay the check if you've done the inviting. The person who invites pays. If a woman invites a man and he asks to share the check, she should decline nicely once; if he insists, let him. A woman should not ask to pay her share if a man has invited her, but she can ask him out for the second date and pay for it.
- Assume responsibility for making the plan. The person who makes the date makes the plan. Asking someone out and then saying, "What would *you* like to do?" is a mistake. You define the date *and* what it will cost you by making a specific plan.
- Be relatively modest and conservative in your choice of an activity and the way you present yourself until you know a person better.
- Keep sensuality low-keyed. Your purpose is to get to know a person, not to seduce him/her.
- Wear clothes you feel comfortable and good in. A date with a new person is no time to try out a new outfit or new shoes.
- Be romantic!

DON'T
- Drink excessively. Drinking very little is the wisest course.
- Haul out a pharmacy of drugs.
- Be provocative in clothes or manner. You're not competing for a role in a soap opera.
- Go to most singles bars and discos—they're too noisy for conversation, and it's conversation that enables you to get acquainted with a new person.
- Complain about how another partner treated you.
- Discuss your personal problems.
- Analyze the other person's problems.

- Dwell on ill health or health problems unless absolutely necessary ("I'm allergic to cigarette smoke"); then only briefly.
- Discuss family or money problems.
- Strain to be witty or humorous—it will come off as artificial.
- Call up someone and say your lonely and then ask for a date.
- Act desperate. A date is just a date, it is not the key to your entire future. Don't cling.
- Discuss any negatives whatsoever, even the bad weather.
- Talk about your diet or exercize program.
- Give details of your allergies, unless absolutely necessary for your comfort (cats, smoking, etc.); then only briefly.
- Sound so casual that you end up vague, as in "Would you like to get together sometime next week and do something?"
- Make an invitation sound like an afterthought as in "I'm not doing anything Friday night, are you?"
- Leave your date hanging while you stand chatting with friends you happen to run into. Make introductions and include him/her in the conversation and keep it brief. You're out with your date, not your buddies.
- Underestimate the impact of your underwear on your mood.
- Do *anything* of which you have even the smallest doubt.

SALLY'S BASIC RULE
When in doubt, *don't*.

Consider the dangers of the Saturday night date. America is hung up on Saturday night. Almost no one *voluntarily* stays home on Saturday night if they have a chance to go out. Ninety percent of us, whether we're sixteen or sixty, think that our social life is a failure if we don't have something planned on Saturday night. Why is this? What's so special about Saturday night?

For one thing, most of us can sleep late on Sunday morning. But that's not the only reason. Traditionally, the work week was much longer and harder than it is now, when more people worked the land. Urban centers were fewer. People had to travel long distances to socialize. And for many it was the only night in the week they took a bath and got cleaned up.

Well, times sure have changed. But old, ingrained attitudes die hard. The Saturday night date is still emotionally loaded. If it's a failure, the week stinks. If it's good, we can get through another work week waiting for the next Saturday night date. Saturday night reminds us of school proms, long dresses, tuxedos, slicked-back hair, corsages, and that anxiey-producing moment at the end of the evening, "Will she or won't she?" and "Should I ask him in?" It's a night fraught with significance.

My advice to the first-dater of any age is, "Don't make it on a Saturday night."

On a Saturday night, you're committed to an evening even if you are bored and know there's no point in going on. A *long* evening. No one can decently cut short a Saturday night at ten—that just screams rejection. Short of breaking your ankle on the curb, there's almost no way out.

Tuesday, however (or any other weeknight) is an entirely different matter. Since most everybody gets up and goes to work, the excuse of having to get up early is valid. On a weekday it is perfectly acceptable to invite someone out for a walk, or a drink, or an ice cream cone, and it's easy to make an excuse when one has suggested a walk. You have to get home and feed the cat, or iron a blouse. Whatever. On the other hand, a satisfactory walk can lead to a cup of coffee, a drink, a longer walk, a late-night snack—can lead to anything. With no pressure. Get my point?

Incidentally, I don't recommend movies for the first date (unless you're painfully shy)—sitting there mum for two hours is no way to get to know a person.

The Sunday brunch is another great way to keep it low-key until you know for sure how much time you want to spend with a person. If you are the guest, you can always bow out gracefully by saying you have a dinner engagement, or an afternoon tea date. The host, by inviting for brunch, limits the encounter if he/she wants to. Both parties can take it from there.

Sexual freedom may abound, but the slow approach still seems to work best. A kiss and a hug are an acceptable way to end an evening, without igniting expectations of something more. If your partner seems to be prodding you in a direction you'd prefer not to go, just say simply and sincerely that you'd like to get to know him/her better because you don't take your sex casually.

With the advent in our lives of sexually transmitted diseases, especially AIDS, it's important for anyone considering a sexual relationship with a new partner to be up front about these vital matters. The day of the slow courtship dance may not be over—it might even be coming back. But the reality of sex today is that it can be a matter of life and death. Unfortunately, most of the responsibility still rests with women, just as birth control has been their primary responsibility. So, if you're a woman, and you're even remotely considering sex, be prepared. Carry condoms, the latex kind, not the natural fibre kind. And insist that the man use one, and use it properly. There's just no other answer today except for abstinence or non-touching sex like mutual masturbation. It's up to you, but it's serious business. Don't let a false sense of modesty stand in the way of protecting yourself. And obviously the place to discuss such matters is not pillow talk. It had better be done and out of the way early in the day.

This doesn't mean that your date has to be any less interesting or exciting in the "getting to know you" phase—it doesn't. What's important is to be aware of the realities and not, ostrich-like, bury your head in the sand hoping the problem will somehow take care of itself. It won't. You have to be aware and prepared to take the proper action. Sexual overtures *must* be straightforward and *honest*. Remember Sally's Basic Rule, "*If in doubt, don't.*" This applies especially to a new sexual partner. And, yes, delaying lovemaking can be a way of heightening mutual interest. Sometimes it is best that not everything is revealed at once. If a man shies away from a frank discussion of "safe sex," it might be an indication that he's not too concerned about his own health, and certainly that he's not worried about protecting yours! It's not unladylike either to ask him if he usually wears condoms. You need to know that *he* knows how to use one correctly. If he's familiar with them, he probably knows his preference. And if neither of you has them and you decide on sex, then go and buy them before going home to bed. And make sure there's a supply. A condom is a one-use item. If you want to make love at night and again in the morning, you'll need two. Or more, depending on the intensity of your lovemaking.

Some men will complain that condoms aren't romantic— but using one doesn't have to be a clumsy operation. The two of you can make a mutual project of it. Remember, no one has been known to recover from AIDS, and women, as receivers of the semen, are the likeliest to get infected, less likely to be transmitters. It's beyond the scope of this book to go into full details of all you need to know about condoms and their use, but there's plenty of quite specific published material available. You are your own responsibility. Do your research. Learn what you need to know.

And don't, under any circumstances, think that "it can't happen to me." It can, it might—if you're not careful.

If your conversation turns to sex, it's okay to hint at your own sexual preferences, but I think it best not to make a point of discussing sex on a first date unless it occurs naturally.

Okay, so you've contracted for that first date—maybe you've even had it already. At some point in the evening, for both parties, comes the unspoken question: how does this end?

If you're a man, you may be thinking about some instant sex, though it's my opinion that men are not so universally quick on the draw as their publicity has made them seem. I've known quite a few who like to test the waters before dipping in. This is not to say that men don't sometimes expect sex from a first date, but I'm talking here about the possibility of a lasting relationship. Men do seem to take the longer view, expecting less from a first date than women usually do. This is no doubt due to the fact that traditionally they are the ones who are the active party in the dating game—they do the asking. If you're a woman, all too often before the evening is out—if it's been a successful one—you have started up your "hope machine," by which I mean the tendency to start weaving marriage fantasies—"Is he *the* one?" This is why the evening's last few words tend to take on monumental importance and start pulsing with expectations.

Take Elaine, for example.

ELAINE: Hi, Sally! It's that time of the morning, isn't it?

SALLY: (Laughing) Well, according to my clock, it's about time to pack it in. What can I do for you?

ELAINE: I don't have a problem. I just wanted to share my excitement and good news with you.

SALLY: Tell me about it.

ELAINE: I'm just so excited—I've finally found the right man and he's just perfect!

SALLY: Hey, wait a minute! How many times have you seen this paragon?

ELAINE: Just once. I just got home from our first date.

SALLY: When is your next date?

ELAINE: Oh, I don't know. He said he'd call tomorrow. Don't you think he will call?

SALLY: I haven't the faintest idea, and neither do you. That's the point.

ELAINE: But he did *say* he'd call.

SALLY: Sure he did. And he may. But it doesn't matter at this point. A first date isn't reality. He may call or he may not. There's no need for you to care. At this point you've invested one evening—a bit, but not a lot. You had a good time. That's enough. Don't expect or ask for more yet. Don't start the hope machine going when you've only spent a few hours with the man. Getting your hopes up on unreality is a sure way to come crashing down.

ELAINE: What should I do if he doesn't call me? Should I call him?

SALLY: Sure, if you want to see him again, you call him. There's nothing wrong in that. But remember that you've got nothing in this relationship yet.

ELAINE: Well, he did say he'd call me.

SALLY: I don't care if he did. Whatever *anybody,* male or female says at the end of a first date is suspect and best ignored. Sometimes people who just mumble off into the dark call bright and early the next morning. But everybody needs a bit of a sorting out period after a first date. For some, it is longer than for others. Nobody really knows what they're saying at the end of a first date.

ELAINE: Sally, that really makes me think. And you're right. I was already wondering which of my friends to ask to be my bridesmaids. (Laughing)

SALLY: There you go. If I've said it once, I've said it a hundred times. Do not listen to anybody's closing line on a first date. Whatever the other party says, ignore it. It's unreality.

ELAINE: Thanks a lot, Sally. I'm really glad I called.

SALLY: Good night.

One of the exclamation points to the non-reality of the male-female relationship is that there is very little—if any—reality in first dates. Think of what happens when they throw up the ball at a basketball game—sure it's important who hits it into whose side of the court to begin the game, but it's no predictor of the outcome. And actually, it doesn't even have anything to do with the game of basketball—it's just one of those rites of passage we've come to expect and it does give a momentary thrill.

So, remember: a disappointing first date has nothing to do with who you are, who the other person is, or what's eventually going to happen in the relationship, which is why I always say, "Go back over the territory." Anybody who was worth a first date—unless it was an unqualified disaster—is worth a second try, because only on a second date will it begin to come into focus what this person's all about.

Getting from the first or second date to commitment is not an easy process. And it needn't be swift. You need time to get to know each other and iron out the little wrinkles. If you are really going for the serious relationship that can go the distance, two years isn't too long a waiting period to make sure you both feel strongly enough to make a commitment. Marry in haste, the poet said, repent at leisure.

Say you've gotten past the "getting to know you" dates, and you feel that this is moving into the serious relationship you've wanted, try my *Fantasy Weekend*.

Invite that "someone special" on a trip to nowhere. Get in the car (or on a bus or train) and take off for an unknown destination. Pack an elegant meal in a picnic basket. I'd take a bottle of champagne, some liver pâté, fresh fruit, cheese, and a nice loaf of crusty bread. Let your own personal tastes dictate the menu. If, for example, you are both chocolate lovers, you could take six kinds of chocolate goodies and just *gorge*. The idea is to have fun, to let yourself indulge *when the mood hits*. Don't be dependent upon finding a Howard Johnson's when you're tired and hungry. Don't have to spend half your evening searching for that "charming restaurant." Be prepared.

If you're driving, pick some easy country roads to visit, and then choose a spot where you can relax and chat, perhaps by a brook or on a grassy knoll. It may seem a contradiction, but you have to work at setting the right mood. You do this by arranging things well in advance and then just letting the magic build.

After your picnic, you'll be relaxed and ready for exploring. Go looking for something different, say a country inn or an old fashioned hotel in a small town. Don't, under any circumstances, pick a standard motel chain.

If you're country folk, do it the other way 'round and go into the nearest big city. Again, the main thing is to just *let it happen*. Be ready to change your mind or your plans if a better idea hits. Follow your mood.

If you're a woman, pack your prettiest gown and robe, your best perfume. If you're a man, take along whatever makes you feel and act most masculine, whether it's a special aftershave lotion or that velvet smoking jacket you got for Christmas and haven't had the nerve to wear yet. Love is always around—you just need a scheme to ensnare it. Taking a chance is often the best way.

A SPECIAL WORD TO MY TEEN-AGE READERS:

We've been talking about dating, but from the calls I get nightly it seems that most younger people are more concerned about going steady than they are about dating.

The tendency today is that younger people, even before they reach their teens, I'm surprised and sad to say, think they have to pick a "true love" and stick with him or her to the exclusion of everyone else.

This is really a big mistake. The girl or boy who has spent all of his or her growing-up years glued to another person exclusively hasn't had a chance to learn about other human beings and how they tick. This can cause real problems when you get to college or into the work force. Even though you may be an adult on the calendar—in your twenties—you'll still be, in many ways, a child inside emotionally.

And if you don't grow up emotionally, you'll be stunted all your life—still be a "boy" or a "girl" instead of maturing into a "man" or a "woman." This "one-true-love-syndrome" seems to be affecting the majority of teens today, and, frankly, I deplore it. Those wonderful years in school should be for *exploration* (and I'm definitely *not* talking about *sexual* exploration, especially with AIDS and other sexually transmitted diseases around). I mean the kind of exploration of getting to know all sorts of different kinds of people—liberal and conservative, fun and serious, intellectual and athletic, and so forth. After all, if you've decided, on the basis of one ice-cream cone, that chocolate is absolutely the only flavor you want or will ever want, you are going to be missing out on the other 99 flavors the ice-cream parlor has to offer—plus the new one every week! More importantly, you won't have the experience to handle the different kinds of people you will run into in college or when working.

Why do kids do this? There may be other reasons, but I think the big one is *security*. Being in love (or convincing yourself you're in love) is a form of security. It's like having a twin—there's always someone there for you, to go to a dance with, to hang out with, to go to the beach with, or whatever. And all the gang knows you're a couple. It's never "Jill" or "Johnny." It's always "Johnny and Jill," almost as if they are the same person.

And that's my point. You're an individual. But you have to develop that individuality. It doesn't just *happen* the way a rosebud becomes a full-blown rose. It takes work and doing. It means overcoming a certain natural shyness and putting yourself out there, testing yourself. This can be difficult—but, believe me, it's worth it. Getting to know a lot of different people may be a bit scary, but it's an adventure and it's *training* for adult life. The problem is that keeping an exclusive bond going for a long time, say five years or more, reinforces any sense of insecurity and uncertainty that may have forged the bond in the first place. The feeling comes in, ''What would I do without him/her?'' And so you hang on even if you'd like to venture forth. It's a false security, and it's no way to build up your own self-confidence, which later on could prove to be a real social handicap.

I know this goes against the current teenage peer pressure, but I also can assure you that if you will get out there on your own you'll be doing yourself a big favor in the long run. You need to be broadening your own experiences, solving your own problems, and doing your own growing up.

You don't have to be in love to date and every date doesn't have to turn into a heartthrob. Dating is a process of discovery—discovering who you are and who the other person is. And dating different people lets you explore different facets of yourself—maybe you enjoy Harry's intellectual approach to life but love Bobby's fun-loving devil-may-care zest. Or perhaps Janey's soft and feminine ways appeal to you but at the same time Sarah's bouncy personality and love of risks intrigues you. The point is, you can experience them *both*, and many more as well. Then, later on when you go to college or to work, you'll have a better idea of who you are, what you like, and this will give you inner confidence, so important in coping in the adult world. So, don't let the crowd pressure you into ''going steady'' so early in life when what you need to be doing is gaining experience. When you are there in the big world, you'll need all the experience you can manage!

PART FIVE

LOOKING
FOR LOVE

17

Looking at Home

WHENEVER THE SUBJECT of love crops up, everyone immediately wonders, "Where do I go to find it?"

It reminds me of a story. A man was walking down a
dark street and up ahead he saw another man walking head
down, in a circle around the street lamp, obviously looking
for something. Wanting to help, the first man asked what
the other had lost. "My house key," was the reply.

So the stroller started to follow the man around in the
circle of lamplight, scrutinizing the ground also. After a
few trips around the lamp post, he asked, "Are you sure
you dropped your key under the lamp?"

"Oh no. I dropped it over there in the garden," was the
reply, accompanied by a gesture toward the dark garden.
"Then why are we looking here?" was the puzzled reply.
"Because there's more light here!"

The point of this story is that often we look in the wrong
place, not because we think that's the place to find what
we're looking for, but because we have a wrong notion
about it all.

The first thing to be aware of is that most people meet
and marry within a ten-mile radius of where they live.

So, if you really want to find love, start looking in your own backyard. Cast aside those romantic notions about love waiting in faraway places. Home is the best place to start looking. You may end up finding love in line at the supermarket!

I cannot emphasize this too much: the more *looking* you do, the better your chances are of *finding*.

A lot of people think that there are times to look and times not to look. Believe me, if you are trying to find love, you must be looking all the time. This means being aware of your surroundings—and who is likely to be in them—and not only looking but *thinking your best*.

Most of us have romantic notions about finding love. We think dreamily of ocean cruises, the sound of guitars, windswept beaches, or the clink of champagne glasses. Our minds run to exotic or unusual circumstances. Women tend to think of moonlight and being swept away by the romantic encounter. Men may fantasize about beautiful girls on sandy beaches or at a fancy party.

Let me give you an example.

Eileen had a subscription to a concert series with a friend. One day her friend called to say she was sick and couldn't go that night. Normally, Eileen wouldn't have gone alone, but this was a concert she had been especially looking forward to, so she decided to go alone. That afternoon she went to the box office to turn in her friend's ticket and she noticed an appealing man standing just in front of her, apparently alone. Ahead of them, an argumentative person was holding up the line, and Eileen made a casual remark about the situation and being in a hurry.

The man smiled sympathetically and mentioned that he was from out of town and had only just heard about the concert. He hoped there would be a good seat available for him.

Eileen said that she had an extra subscription seat—that he was welcome to buy her friend's ticket; it was an excellent seat. He thanked her, paid for the ticket, and they parted.

That night they met in their seats and chatted about the music during intermission. After the concert, Eileen suggested that they might enjoy a cup of coffee together. They exchanged business cards, and the next week he called her in her office to say he would be in town again that week and would like to invite her this time to another concert.

You see? Eileen dared to talk to a stranger who happened to share her interest, and romance bloomed.

Or, suppose you don't have an extra concert ticket handy? What to do? How to bridge the gap between conversation and moving toward a date or meeting? *Invent a party!*

Schedule to leave for Europe in a few weeks, my friend Tara had suddenly discovered her passport was expired. Ticket in hand, she rushed down to the Passport Office. She's an outgoing woman, and she was wearing a zany hat. Bored with waiting in line, she began chatting away with the people standing near her.

Then she spotted a large, handsome man *reading a music score*. That *really* sparked her interest. But suddenly she felt shy. How in the world could she make contact in a public room? Though she was chatting with a group of several people near her, he was down the line a bit, even though the snake-shape of the line brought him right next to her when it moved.

She could tell that he was interested in her—his eyes would wander to the group around her, all were talking animatedly, enjoying themselves. What if *he's* shy, she thought? Maybe he wants to make contact, but doesn't know how. *It's up to me!* With her back to the crowded room she took out one of her personal cards, which had her name and phone number on it (but not her address).

When she had finished at the counter, she saw that she would pass him as she was leaving and she began feeling shy again. To bolster her courage she said to herself, "Sally told me to do this."

She stopped in front of him.

"You must be the only person here who, because some-one said, 'It's a long line, take a book,' brought a music score."

Smiling, he said, "I've got a lot of music to learn in a short time."

"Oh? Are you a musician? A conductor? A singer?"

"A singer. I'm singing in an opera in just two weeks."

"Which role?"

"Baritone."

"Is that why you're on the passport line—are you sing-ing abroad?"

"Not this one. But I'm doing a concert tour in July."

Tara knew a considerable amount about opera (see what I mean about interest?) and they continued talking about different roles and singers, but she was at a loss as to how to make the overture. But where there's a will there's an idea.

Suddenly she said, "You know, you seem such an interesting person. I'm giving a party soon and I'd like to invite you. I'm sure you'd enjoy my friends. One of them is a soprano."

"I'd like to come."

"Good. Here, take my card and give me a call when you have a chance. I'm in most afternoons."

"I'd love to. By the way, my name's Nick."

"Great. I look forward to hearing from you."

Now, Tara hadn't actually *planned* a party—but what the heck? On her way home she thought of a small guest list and a menu—she knew some close friends who could be counted on to make time for an impromptu party, especially when she told them the delightful story of how she'd met Nick!

By taking a quite small chance, Tara had scored. And

by her clever inventing of a party, she had overstepped the awkward first date and arranged for her friends to scrutinize him simultaneously. When he called, she could suggest they meet for afternoon coffee to further check him out, but she was safe in inviting a stranger to her home because her friends would be there too.

Tara's quick thinking was the result of being aware of the possibilities—and of always being on the lookout for love.

SALLY'S BASIC RULE

Be prepared. That's the best way not to fumble when opportunity presents itself. It's a good idea to *always* carry personal cards, attractively designed, with your name and phone number only. A personal card gives you instant access to another person in a non-threatening way. You risk nothing. And at the crucial moment, nobody has to hunt for pen and paper.

So, at-home love possibilities abound. As I've said, do your homework. *Research.* Get in there and dig out the possibilities. Sitting home by the TV munching potato chips will not get you the love you claim you want.

Neither will whining that "there's nothing to do in this town." (And if you really *have* exhausted all the possibilities your town has to offer, go at once to the chapter called "Looking on Weekends.")

You have to know people and constantly meet new people. If your circle of friends is the old gang from high school or college, you may very well be justified in your feeling that there's nothing new on the horizon.

Keep in touch with the events that your town has to offer—look for ideas in your local newspaper and on bulletin boards—almost every supermarket and church has a community bulletin board. Community centers, shopping malls, and colleges that cater to adult night classes also offer events that will increase your chances of meeting new people. Read the social and entertainment pages of every newspaper in town.

Visibility is the clue. Sitting home won't do it. And every town, no matter how small (well, maybe not if it's population is 212), has various organizations and associations. A library. A museum. Music. Athletics. Seminars. Classes. If you're in a university town, go to the school and check around. Get a catalog of the adult classes. Many cities now have organizations that sponsor classes in just about anything you could want to learn. Check it out.

Today the health or fitness club seems to be replacing the bar as a meeting place, especially among the younger set. So, whether you need it or not (and most of us need it), consider a membership in a health or fitness club.

Language classes are good, too. Again, even if you don't manage to find love through one of them, you will enhance your chances on your next vacation. And which of us isn't made to feel better and more confident by the ability to speak another language?

A word of caution here: for some reason, the sexes seem to gravitate toward different languages. Women tend to study Italian, Spanish, French; men tend to study Arabic, Chinese, Russian. The implication is clear—if you are a woman wanting to meet men, choose one of these far-flung global languages; if a man wanting to meet women, choose a European language.

Sporting events are a mixed bag, with basketball, hockey and softball good bets for women looking for men, and tennis matches, sailing events and swim meets a good way for men to meet women. Nonprofessional sports such as little league baseball draw a big crowd of men—lots of the little boys who are playing in the game will have daddies who are divorced.

I know that the bar scene isn't for everyone—but I must confess that my Aunt Carrie met her first two husbands at bars, so I can't discount them entirely. I prefer a family-owned local restaurant, where you can get to know the owner. A restaurant is different, but has some of the friendliness of a bar; it's an especially good bet. It really depends on your temperament and tastes. If you don't freqent bars, there's no need to start now, but if you do, be aware that they can be a help in your quest for love, if you choose the right places.

Singles bars, however, usually are bad places to find love. They are geared to sex, attract a lot of men who are just looking for a night out on the town, and are often filled with "the walking wounded"—those who are still suffering the trauma of a recent divorce or a breakup and are out more for instant soothing in the form of a one-night stand than real love. I suggest avoiding them.

By hanging out in your local pub or bar—thereby making yourself visible—you're making it clear that you're looking for love. That's good—but it's not enough. Let *everybody* know that you are looking for love. Tell your friends. Tell your relatives. Don't miss a one, not even ninety-three-year-old Great Aunt Winnie—you never know who will wander through her ken.

Take Greg. He was looking for love but he hadn't bothered to tell his Great Aunt Katharine, whom he visited dutifully twice a week. One day Aunt Katharine noticed he seemed a bit down in the dumps, and she asked why. Greg confessed he was unhappy in his loveless although successful life, and Aunt K. "took it under advisement," as they say in business circles. A couple of weeks later she mentioned Priscilla and invited Greg to tea to meet the young lady. Greg went, but only out of duty—who in the world could old Aunt K. know? Some drippy loser, no doubt, who he'd have to be polite to for an afternoon. Oh, well, he thought, at least Aunt K. made a smashingly good nut cake and plum torte.

The day came and an unenthusiastic Greg journeyed across town to Aunt K.'s for the proposed tea. There he found a vision of loveliness named Priscilla. Turned out that Cilla (as she was called) was a veterinarian, newly practicing in Aunt K.'s neighborhood. She'd responded to a call regarding the health of Aunt K.'s old poodle and, in caring for the dog, had struck up a friendship with Aunt K., who targeted her for her handsome, sad nephew.

A dumbfounded Greg discovered Cilla much more interesting than even Aunt K.'s plum torte. Amazed that his ancient relative could be so savvy, and keep such fine company, he lingered until tea turned into cocktails and then took the two ladies out to dinner. Greg and Cilla have been dating since, and when Aunt K.'s old poodle finally went to his just reward, they presented her with a darling replacement puppy, in gratitude, and, as Greg said, "To keep the connection."

Here's a checklist of suggested activities with indications of which ones are good for men to meet women and vice versa:

Activity	Meet Men	Meet Women
Competitions, such as chess or badminton	X	
Auctions	X	X
Art gallery openings		X
Garage/yard sales	X	X
Wine tasting	X	
Cooking classes		X
Camera clubs	X	X
Stock brokerage classes	X	
Saturday mornings at bike-repair shops	X	

Activity	Meet Men	Meet Women
Concerts in the park	X	X
Friends, relatives *(very important: everybody likes to be a matchmaker)*	X	X
Health clubs	X	X
Little theatre groups		X
Little league baseball	X	
Golf tournaments	X	
Dog/cat shows		X
Sporting goods shops	X	
Auto racing	X	
Marathoning	X	X
Political clubs	X	X
Theatrical events	X	X
Special interest clubs	X	X
Professional organizations	X	X
Flea markets	X	X
Advocacy organizations	X	X
Mayor's committees	X	X
Church groups	X	X
Hiking clubs	X	
Women's study programs		X
University classes	X	X
Local option courses	X	X
Flying lessons	X	
Target practice	X	
Lectures	X	X
Traveling exhibits	X	X
Conventions	X	X
Collectors' meetings	X	X
Crafts fairs	X	X
PTA meetings		X
Parents Without Partners	X	X
Adult education courses	X	X
Local boat basins	X	

| TV show audiences | X | X |
| Library programs | X | X |

Research your own town and neighborhood for more ideas.

A word about dating services. So far, I have not heard of a *single* person who has had a satisfactory relationship as the result of a dating service, so I don't recommend them. If you try one, do let me know if you have any success.

The new radio hot-lines that put people together have received mixed reviews from my audiences, but the general response has been good.

Classified ads seem to be much more workable, perhaps because *you* do the choosing instead of someone else choosing for you. The options are more in the control of the person who runs an ad or answers one. Don't be shy about it—and remember what I said about finding your personal style and preference . . . so that you can write the ad that best describes *you*. A word of caution if you advertise in a national publication. Make sure that you state your geographical location and obtain the location of a prospective partner. It's happened that couples have corresponded and talked by telephone for weeks, or even months, and felt they had much in common—but he lived on a ranch in Montana and she was a schoolteacher in Georgia. Neither had the money or time to bridge the geographical gap. Be sure to consider your resources and your ability to travel across long distances before getting involved through the personals ads with someone not in your immediate area.

Also, while looking for love at home, follow the Rules of Action and Visibility: the more you see, the more you are seen, the wider your network of social contacts, the broader the horizon of your opportunities to find love.

18

Looking on the Job

Is IT A good idea to date someone you work with?

I know all the objections—most people feel that you *shouldn't* date on the job, but, being ornery, I take another stand.

I say: Yes, it's a good idea to date someone you work with.

I think the advantages outweigh the possible disadvantages. Let's first take a look at the disadvantages:

1. Some companies frown on office romances, even to the extent that if two people in the company marry, one must leave. However, isn't it better to find love and find another job? Of course, if a major career is involved, this is something to take into consideration. Again, it's a matter of setting priorities.

2. If the affair breaks up, there is the problem of having to face that person every day on the job. If this is too much for you, you may have to consider leaving the job. But the chances are that if the job is truly satisfying it will be a source of solace to you. And if it isn't that satisfying, it's probably time to move on anyway.

3. The person in the subordinate position may get fired. This happens especially to women, but the shoe can get on the other foot. Take Ben. He was having an affair with his boss's secretary at the computer firm where he was employed as a technician. After a few weeks, she decided to break it off, for reasons she declined to discuss with Ben. Naturally, he was upset.

   He pursued her even after he cornered her in the coffee room and told her off, with some rather unflattering remarks. Three days later, his boss called him in and fired him.

   It was only afterward that he learned that the girl had decided the boss was better pickin's.

So it isn't always the woman who pays if the romance goes sour. But Ben's story isn't typical. It's usually the woman who is left out in the cold without a job when an affair ends acrimoniously, especially if it's been with her boss.

Whatever your sex, before you get into an office romance, remember to plan ahead a bit for the end, because you're going to have to deal with that person every day. If the person you break up with can do you any harm, then there's no point in getting nasty or difficult (as Ben unwisely did). The smart thing to do, if you've lost the love, is to try to keep the job! As always, preparation and planning are great tools for keeping life running smoothly in the face of trauma.

But let's look at the *bright* side of love on the job.

As I've said, there are plenty of advantages. One is that being in love at work makes the day sing, especially if you've got a job that's difficult or a bit boring. Just knowing you're going to have a few quick moments with your love, possibly lunch or coffee, makes the day brighter.

This way, too, you have an automatic confidant with whom you can discuss job problems, someone already

interested in your job and its details. Shoptalk may bore a
lover who hasn't the foggiest idea of what you're talking
about but two people who work together have a shorthand
that makes everything easier. Also, a lover who is in
another field of endeavor is naturally going to want to talk
about his/her job as well, and though allotting equal time
to such discussions is democratic, it's more satisfying if
both are interested in the same cast of characters. You
don't have to keep explaining that Sue is Bill's assistant
and Jim is Joe's boss and so forth.

One of the best ways to find love on the job is to work
for a big company. If you are now considering a job
change, or going for a first job, or a new one, do consider
how the workplace affects your opportunities for finding
love.

Big corporations tend to have a lot of employee
activities—yearly picnics, staff meetings, seminars, extra-
curricular courses, a company cafeteria or lunch room.
These are all excellent places to meet others, and you have
a built-in topic of conversation. It's so easy to plunk your
lunch tray down next to that handsome man or pretty
woman you've been eyeing and say, "Hi! I'm Joe/Jane.
I'm in Sales. I've seen you around but I don't know your
name." Right away, you're off and running.

Is it advisable to change jobs in order to find love?

Women in particular are affected by this question. Now,
you can read all these books and buy the philosophy that
today your own path and the career on the job should be
terribly important to you, as it has traditionally been to
men. This is okay—in fact, I buy the philosophy myself.
But the *reality* of the situation is that a great many women,
even those who are liberated, strong, and successful, begin
to feel a kind of emptiness at a certain time in their lives.
This usually hits in the late twenties and early thirties,
after they've established themselves in the job or career,

but before the concern about the biological clock running down comes in.

A typical call I had was from Elizabeth in Phoenix.

SALLY: Hi!

ELIZ.: Hi! Sally, I'm a first-time caller.

SALLY: Nice to meet you.

ELIZ.: I wanted to talk to you about something important.

SALLY: Shoot.

ELIZ.: Well, I was transferred here to Phoenix by my company a year and a half ago. I've got a really good job and the transfer was a promotion. I'm in middle management and I'm being groomed for a higher level. I've been working ten years, and in ten years I've changed jobs four times and now I think I've found one that's right for me, where I can develop and use my talents.

SALLY: Sounds good to me. What's the problem?

ELIZ.: I'm lonely.

SALLY: Why do you think you're lonely?

ELIZ.: Well, I'm really doing okay in the job. And I've made some friends here. But what's worrying me is that I've been thinking a lot now about having someone in my life—that significant other, you know what I mean? (Laughing)

SALLY: Yes, I do. You need some romance, right?

ELIZ.: Right. And I can tell you that there is just nobody in this town for me. I've been here long enough to check out the situation pretty thoroughly and it's totally dismal. I just don't find any prospects. Right now I'm thinking about changing jobs again to get myself to an area where I'd have a better chance to meet someone right for me. Is that crazy?

SALLY: Not necessarily. Do you think it's crazy?

ELIZ.: Well, I'm making $28,000 now—and I never thought I'd make that much money. And it's a good job. But I'm just not happy anymore.

SALLY: Then you have to do something about it. Priorities shift as we go through life. Sounds as if you've now decided that having somebody is equally as important as earning $28,000, being a middle-management person. And prioritizing is what it's all about.

ELIZ.: Then you think it's okay for me to change jobs again?

SALLY: Sure, it's okay. If what's important to you now is finding love, and if you've researched a good place to go for that purpose—you can afford to take a job paying a few thousand less for a while. Money isn't everything, is it?

My feeling is that though money and a career are very important to a woman, and might possibly last longer than romance, if you've decided that right now the top priority in your life is finding love, you should go for it. Shifting jobs won't totally upset your life. After all, mobility on the job is the American way. That's how we do it.

First of all, consider the value of your job to your life. If you live in an area where jobs are plentiful and you have some choice, you're in a good situation. But if you don't have much choice, be careful. Are you happy in your job? Remember that being unhappy with your job will not enhance your ability to find love.

Naturally, if you're in a one-of-a-kind job—if you're president of a college or going to star in a movie—the choice is pretty clear. Unless it's really making you miserable, and then it's back to setting priorities.

Take Sam, who called me one night in despair over his love life. Divorced for a few years, he had been having a very hard time meeting women because he worked as a garage mechanic at a garage that serviced heavy trucks. All day long, day in and day out, he saw nothing but male truck drivers. Not much chance of romance there! Still,

Sam liked being a mechanic. It paid good money, let him enjoy the finer things of life off duty, allowed him to take vacations he enjoyed, and paid for his nice car and pleasant apartment filled with stereo and electronic equipment.

Should he change his job, he wondered? And if so, to what?

I advised Sam to change his *job* but not his field. Any good car mechanic is going to be in demand. I suggested he do his research to find out which garages were in neighborhoods where single women might be bringing their cars for servicing. After a couple of weeks of checking around, he applied at a garage near a community college which taught many adult extension courses to women reentering the job market or seeking new skills.

His record was outstanding, and he was hired. The new management thought that they had gotten a bargain because they paid a couple of dollars less an hour than the heavy-duty truck place, but Sam was satisfied when he saw all those nicely dressed women bringing their cars in for servicing! In one bold stroke he had widened his opportunities to meet the kind of women he liked. He was so good at diagnosing their mechanical troubles he became an instant hero.

Some of his male clients followed him to the new place, too, and before long Sam had increased his salary back to what it had been before. Everything was the same, only now he was surrounded by women and talking to them every day. Now Sam's dating Joy, a teaching assistant who is working on her degree. And Joy's car has never run better!

Women have a higher mobility ratio than men when it comes to changing jobs, because many are lower paid and therefore have less to lose, or because they have been traditionally less career-oriented than men. But as men free themselves from the stereotype of profession-as-identity, they too will become more mobile.

A woman working in an all-woman office, or only with one or two married men for bosses, with few outside opportunities to meet men would be wise to look around for a position more conducive to finding love. So consider a change to give yourself ample opportunities to find love.

Back to Ben for a moment. He got fired for his passion, but after a period of licking his wounds and thinking the woman was unnecessarily vindictive, he got himself together and went out and found a job that better suited his talents.

Later he told me that getting fired was the best thing that could have happened to him. He had been sort of drifting along in the job anyway, enlivened by love-on-the-job. After talking to me he set his sights on a job that would be in a less male-dominated atmosphere.

Another case is Gary, from, of all places, Indiana. Gary called me one night and told me this story:

An executive for a trucking firm, Gary liked his job fine. In fact, he'd just been promoted and was making $85,000 yearly. The trouble was that he never met any women. He'd been divorced for five years and was getting pretty lonely and fed up with the all-masculine world he inhabited.

Naturally, I couldn't advise Gary to change his job—but I did advise him to start *using* its many possibilities, as well as to investigate the ideas I've just given in ''Looking at Home.''

Work-related activities such as meetings, trade shows, associations, unions, conferences, conventions can be valuable adjuncts to the search for love.

And now, let's go on to the exploration of that idea in ''Looking on Business Trips.''

19

Looking on Business Trips

A FRIEND OF mine, Sharon, who travels a lot for business has developed this trick: when she finds herself alone in a strange town, she picks out a good restaurant with a lively bar that is close to her hotel.

Instead of accepting a table for one at the rear near the kitchen door, which is where single people are often seated, Sharon insists on being seated at a table in the bar area. This way, she is part of the action without feeling like she's a pickup. She's able to share in the lively atmosphere of the bar scene while enjoying her dinner and even catching up on a bit of paperwork left over from her work day.

While true love has never come her way using this method, she has often had wine sent to her from an admirer sitting at the bar. She's also had interesting conversations with men who have asked to join her at the table. She's been kept from many an otherwise lonely evening, and she plans to continue to use this ploy as one of her strategies for finding love.

Looking for love on business trips is an extension of looking at home—except, obviously, that you are not at home, and this has many advantages. For one thing, most of us seem to be a bit more relaxed when we are away from daily responsibilities and duties. We have more free time, even if it's a busy day workwise. In the evenings, unless you're a true workaholic who spends the entire time in his/her room doing paperwork, we're usually up for some relaxing fun. There are usually new things to experience.

Having interests plays along with meeting new people—if you concentrate totally on work you'll be less likely to have interesting conversations, unless you happen on someone who is nuts about your work.

Let me tell you a story.

Karen and Barbara went on a three-day convention as buyers with a local department store. Afterward, Barbara told me Karen had met a dozen men, gone out for dinner every night, and had arranged for a couple of continuing relationships. What was wrong with *her?*

After asking Barbara a few questions about herself and Karen, what became clear was that Barbara didn't know what she was looking for, was not sure it was "correct" to meet a man at a business occasion, and always worried that it might be inconvenient. As a result, she appeared to be unapproachable. For looking on business trips (and elsewhere) I suggest you follow:

SALLY'S BASIC RULE

Look like you are looking. Being approachable is a big part of being approached. Be smiling and friendly. Don't take refuge in a book or business magazine. Let your eyes roam.

Both sexes tend to make themselves less-than-approachable on business trips. Women tend to fear being thought a pick-up (absolutely not necessarily so, ladies), and men tend to wrap themselves up in their work because it passes time.

Karen told me about Jim, whom she had met on a recent business trip to St. Paul, Minnesota. Although Karen always carries work she can do on the airplane if there's no one interesting around, she always waits before taking it out to be sure there's not someone she'd like to talk to. This trip was no exception. Jim was sitting next to her. Karen is looking for love and she is looking all the time, and she's always smiling and friendly, ready to go wherever the encounter leads. She opened up the conversation by asking Jim if he were going to St. Paul/Minneapolis.

"Yes," he replied, smiling in return. "I make this trip often."

"You do?" she asked. "My company's opening a branch there."

After chatting a while, Karen learned that Jim was a frequent flyer and, following the rule that people like to talk about their vacations, she asked what he was planning to do with his frequent-flyer bonus. Jim said he was planning a trip on the Orient Express.

You'll remember we said earlier that *interests* were the key to conversation gambits and keeping things going beyond the initial "how are you?" and "what business are you in?" type of talk.

Karen told Jim that she was a railroad buff and that she'd been reading up on the Orient Express and how an American had reclaimed it from ruin. He was fascinated by her knowledge and thrilled that she was interested in what for him was to be a very special vacation. By trip's end, they were making plans to get together back on the home turf and he had offered to show her around St. Paul/Minneapolis to help her get acquainted with the town.

A word here to women travelers: it *is* sensible to be concerned about safety. Many women (like Barbara) shy away from making contacts on trips because there is an element of fear. It's always safe to talk to someone sitting next to you on a plane or a train. A conversation in neutral surroundings—with accessible topics like destinations and reasons for the trip—offers ample opportunity to judge a person's character. And remember that all flights aren't *vacation* flights. Whenever possible, when traveling for business take the usual business flights. Businessmen are serious travelers and will usually welcome the diversion of a woman companion.

Margie was traveling to San Francisco on business in June, and her seatmate happened to be another woman. Using the exact same approach as she would have if her seat companion had been a man (we are talking about using friendliness in a general way, without overt sexual tones), she struck up a conversation. Margie was looking for love, not a new woman friend, but she knew from experience that one thing leads to another.

Later on, once they had returned to their home city, the two women got together for lunch and still later Margie was invited to attend her friend's brother's birthday party. When Margie was introduced, the friend said jokingly to her brother, "This is Margie. She's your birthday present from me."

It was no joke. Now Margie is married to the birthday boy!

If Margie had not had enough interests in her life to establish a common ground with a woman she wouldn't ordinarily have pursued for friendship, she would have missed meeting the brother—and her husband-to-be. She could have, seeing no male prospects about, turned to her book or her work. But she didn't. You have to be *constantly* aware and looking to expand your social horizons in every direction. Business trips are excellent ways to do this.

Whether you are male or female, try to fly first class, especially on flights that might also be carrying vacationers. Naturally, if your company does not allow first-class expense, this can be a problem. But if the difference is not too great and you can pay it, do so at least once in a while, especially on longer flights. From my experience, it seems that there are more people of the right age and availability in first class. Also, look into possibilities of getting "upgraded," which means you are seated in business or first class on an economy ticket. Some airlines have a policy of doing this regularly with their frequent fliers, when seats in a better class are not booked. Ask about this.

If you can't manage first-class passage, you can join any major airline's VIP Club for a small fee, under $75 a year. There you can sit and hobnob with the first-class flyers and enter the airplane from the first-class door, even if you do have to go on back to economy. Sometimes if you've struck up a conversation with a first-class passenger, he or she may ask the purser to invite you into first class. This has happened to any number of people I know. One girlfriend of mine met a gentleman in the VIP lounge, and when he discovered she wasn't flying first class with him, he offered to pay the difference in her fare. Being a liberated woman, she declined, but after takeoff she saw him sauntering down the aisle toward her seat with a bottle of champagne. *He* joined *her!*

Here are some tips for finding love on business trips:

- Always stay in a business hotel in town.
- Business people like to meet each other.
- Men on the road like to instruct women on the road; chivalry is *not* dead.
- Women travelers are not considered "easy" if they make and accept dates while traveling.
- Any question about business traveling is an appropriate conversation opening line. ("How does one get to town from the airport?" "Is there a gym in the Hotel Na-

tional?'' ''How long a ride is it from the airport to downtown?'' ''Do you know some good restaurants?'')

- Don't stay in your room. Check in, leave your baggage, and go have a look around.
- It's perfectly all right for a woman to go to the bar of a traveler's hotel without being conspicuous. Take a notebook and your pen or magazine, but don't take a book.
- Pick the largest hotel in town.
- Avoid motels whenever possible.
- For safety, women can ask for a room near the elevator bank. If you are assigned a room a long walk down a corridor from the elevator, ask for a different room. Explain.
- Go to any convention you can possibly get to.
- Schedule your travel to coincide with any large event, such as a convention or organizational meeting.
- Read a business paper daily.
- If you're new in a town and on business, try not to leave the hotel in the evening, as you are more likely to meet others who are single in the hotel's dining rooms, lounges, bars, and lobby.
- Know as much as possible about the city you are going to visit beforehand. Get a newspaper when you arrive to check events; it will provide topics of conversation.
- Always write the company or people you are going to do business with and let them know your schedule.
- Make it a point to let drop your single status and that you are open to meeting and dating while on your business trip. For example, when you telephone your business contact to confirm an appointment, you might say something like this:

"Hi, Ed. I'm here and we'll be getting together tomorrow, but I've got some free time before we meet. Since I'm single, I wonder if you have any ideas where I might go for a nice time?''

There's absolutely nothing wrong with asking social advice of a business person. They are knowledgeable about their town and its activities. Also, if you let them know you're single, you give them the opportunity to invite you on a personal basis. You never know whether your business contact has a sister/brother/cousin/niece/nephew or whatever that they might be dying to fix up with you! Many a businessman's wife, faced with her husband's client, wonders if he is married and if she dares introduce her single sister or girlfriend at a dinner party. Take them off the hook. People generally like to be helpful, especially to out-of-towners. Let them.

I've been asked by many women: when traveling, how do you tell if a man is married? *Ask him!* Don't beat around the bush. Few men will lie in the face of the direct question. Also, it puts the matter up front where it belongs. You don't have to spend an evening wondering if you are getting involved with a married man. He doesn't have to think that you are just out for a little casual sex. It's clear from the beginning.

Men, too, can ask forthrightly if there is any question, though most married women still wear their wedding rings. However, an unmarried woman could have a serious relationship at home, and it's entirely proper to find out. "Are you married or involved with someone?" lets the woman know you are hoping for a relationship and sets things off on the right foot.

- Keep a file of contacts. The more people you know and can reach out to in towns you travel to on business, the happier a time you'll have when the business day is over. My friend Marion keeps a separate address book for each town she visits and each book includes even people who are no longer business contacts for her (because they changed jobs, married, or work in a different field). When she gets to town, she gives them all a call, just to let them know she's around and still single. So, she's rarely dateless when traveling.

Here's a special tip: "Women's Guides" to different cities are now available, offering a wonderful fund of information about what is going on in each city. Every topic, from fashion to child care, is covered, and among the general sources are listed organizations and groups which can be contacted by the visitor. Men, too, could benefit from reading these books. City magazines, too, are helpful resource books. They are usually available in hotel lobbies, but if you don't see one, ask.

An artist friend of mine, Bill, was going off to Philadelphia on business and I offered to loan him the *Women's Guide to Philadelphia*. In it he found an association called Women in Graphic Arts. He contacted them and discovered they held a dinner every first Tuesday. When he explained that he was a graphic artist in Philadelphia, was single, and knew no one, he was immediately welcomed and met a whole bevy of women artists. Now when he goes to Philly on business, he has plenty of women to ask for dates.

These women's groups are all willing to offer the visiting woman advice and guidance, friendliness and help. Almost any interest you have can be found in one of these books.

The networking club is another route to follow if you're looking for love on a business trip. There are several of these organizations in different cities. Membership usually requires business-type dress and there is a modest fee (from $5.00 to $15.00) for admission. Most clubs meet at a popular hangout place—a restaurant or a disco. Everyone exchanges business cards (be sure you have a good supply on hand).

Listed below are some of these groups that especially welcome business travelers.

Atlanta: The Atlanta Business Network sponsors 25 activities a month, from breakfasts to happy hours. Call Alan Mitchell, 404 435-1154.

Boston: Networking Unlimited meets every Monday at the Government Center Holiday Inn. Call 617 893-2310.

Dallas: The Library Club gathers for sunset hours at Bryan Tower every weeknight. Attendance is by invitation only. For information, call Tom Jaco, 214 745-1031.

Greenwich, Conn.: The Business Card Club hosts dances at country clubs. Call Russell Pruner, 203 629-1878.

Los Angeles: Every other Wednesday, one YES branch parties at Tiberio's; the other at the L. A. Athletic Club. Call 213 657-5500.

New York: Mimi and Jerry Rubin's Network Party—the pioneer—swings every Tuesday at the Palladium dance club. Call 212 245-6555.

20

Looking on Weekends

HAVE YOU EVER thought of just taking off for a wild weekend to Paris on the chance that you might find love there?

Do it!

Open your P.W.S.A. (Paris Weekend Savings Account) now. One day you'll go, and it might be the thrill of your life.

In the meantime, consider how you can spend your weekends more economically looking for love *nearby*. Within a 100-mile radius of where you're sitting right now (unless you're in the Mojave desert or on the polar icecap), you'll find a host of intriguing possibilities for finding love.

For this book, we researched a typical American city for possibilities, and we're glad we did. We found an amazing number of them (Minneapolis/St. Paul was our sample city). We discovered places that even the natives didn't know existed! There are peaceful rivers, lakes and backroads, historic sites that go back to the nineteenth century to the days when the early settlers were making inroads into the wilderness. We traced back to the first trappers, traders, lumbermen, and settlers—and learned some American history in the process. Not only did we find innumerable places to go in the area, good for the seeker for love, but we added some important interests and extra knowledge to our store as well.

Everyone has chores on weekends. But a mite of planning—an echo here to what we have been advising all along—will go a long way toward activating your weekend time for productive use in the finding of love.

Here's a short list to help you:

- Resort hotels
- Business hotels
- Sports weekends
- Weekend meetings of various sorts
- Seminars and educational group meetings
- Yoga weekends
- Dude ranches
- Weekend conferences on a variety of topics
- Church and other organizational trips
- Special interest towns
- Art and music festivals

That's by no means the extent of things we found in Minneapolis/St. Paul. We also discovered that the local people are always eager to help. No one we asked for information refused it. In fact, we found that asking people for help about their area led to many new acquaintances. Bear in mind also that looking on weekends need not mean an entire weekend out of town. There are always pleasant day trips that don't require an overnight stay.

Call or write to the chamber of commerce of the town or towns you think might be interesting. They will tell you what the town's calendar of events is, and make suggestions about places to visit and stay. Find out what might be attracting tourists to the area. They are going to be eager to meet new people too. Whatever event you choose to center your weekend around, be open to meeting and greeting people. *Talk*—to everyone you meet. Any sort of activity—even asking for directions—can give you a perfect chance to speak to strangers. Ask questions, make comments, offer opinions. Bone up on the town—you can always get a newspaper when you arrive or in advance. Think about the seasonal possibilities—berry picking, for example.

Outside Minneapolis is Cambridge—a short drive. Yearly there's an Annual Swedish Festival in mid-June. A manure spreader race is just one of this festival's hilarious events where everyone talks to everyone else and laughs at the contestants. In the winter, there are curling matches, held weekly on the Isanti County Fairgrounds from December through March. A curling club meets several nights a week in winter.

In Montgomery, in late July, there's a wonderful festival called Kolacky Days. A *kolacky* is a sweet pastry filled with fruit preserves. During the festival these distinctive confections are honored, and other ethnic foods are available, too. There is a queen pageant and parade, polka dancing, and dancers in authentic Czech costumes. Near the festival is a charming old-fashioned inn with twelve rooms, for overnight guests.

The Minneapolis/St. Paul area offers ample opportunity to meet people and find love. Just hours away are museums, festivals, a cheese farm, historic sites, boat tours, canoeing, wildlife preserves, parks, an opera theater, and even a wonderful Renaissance fair. Incidentally, this type of thing is something that's getting quite popular all over the country. People go to dress up in the garb of another century and recreate that time. It's wonderful fun and you can participate as well as be a spectator.

In August and September, the Minnesota Renaissance Faire transforms two hundred acres of woodland into a rollicking festival filled with troubadors, jugglers, musicians, magicians, and other performers roaming the grounds.

Craftspeople come from near and far to sell their wares, which are reproductions of the things of the period. There are food and drink and a merry atmosphere. If I lived in or around Minneapolis, I wouldn't miss it.

These few examples—by no means exhaustive—will give you an idea of how many possibilities you can turn up in your area. Do your homework. Go to the library and get some travel books about your area. Check the publication *Where,* which is a visitor's guide published in major cities across the nation. When you arrive at your weekend destination, go to the visitor's bureau or the lobby of a large hotel and buy a few of the small newspapers offering information about local events. It's best, of course, to do your research in advance, but if a spontaneous mood hits you and you decide to strike out for parts unknown without a specific plan, get information when you hit town.

Stay away from couples resorts. Ski family weekends, for example, aren't good. Neither are little country inns, unless they are connected with a special event, as in our sample above. Single weekends at big resort hotels, I'm told, can be very disappointing. They tend to have the meat-rack atmosphere of the bars.

Pick activities at which you either excel or with which you feel comfortable. If you don't know how to ski, unless you are really prepared to take plenty of lessons, a ski resort would be a bad choice. Skiers are usually serious about their sport, and the neophyte might not feel at ease with the experts. Of course, if you *like* just sitting by the fire and sipping grog, there's always plenty of camaraderie "après-ski."

If you feel shy or insecure in a bathing suit, don't pick a swimming resort. Draping yourself around a pool and trying to keep your body covered is a waste of time, money and energy—choose a weekend on which you can be happily clothed.

Clothes are important, too, but above all, they should be comfortable. Weekend trips are not the time to try out a fancy, new wardrobe—you should feel comfortable, relaxed in what you are wearing. Research is called for in this area as well. Find out what the appropriate clothing is for where you are going. Ask a travel agent or someone who's been there. A book store can furnish you with data. Just ask the clerk to help you find out about the adjacent area. If you've always gone to one or two places, branch out. Do something different.

Alone or with someone? That's up to you. Many men and women feel more at ease when they have a companion. Make sure that you and your companion are in agreement about the purpose of the trip. If you're a woman, for example, *do* tell your traveling friend that you are looking for love. Don't pick someone who will feel deserted if you find it and she doesn't. Make definite arrangements and stick to them—you can agree, for instance to have breakfast and dinner together, or you can leave dinner open, depending on what happens. Have an alternate plan for transportation if one of you happens to want to stay an extra day. When you travel with a friend, it is important that you be clear with each other about what to do if one of you finds love.

What is the secret fear some people have about traveling alone?

Phyllis is typical. She had heard me talking about the advisability of taking weekend trips to broaden one's social life.

PHYLLIS: Hi, Sally. I wanted to talk to you about something you said the other night, about taking trips alone.
SALLY: Okay. What about it?
PHYLLIS: Well, I just can't see myself going on a trip alone.

SALLY: Why not? Have you ever done it?

PHYLLIS: (Laughing self-consciously) Goodness, no!

SALLY: Then that's the problem. It's always that first-time jitters. You know, I've never had anyone call me and say they've taken four major trips alone and still hate the idea of traveling alone.

PHYLLIS: I guess I'd better tell you I'm a bit older.

SALLY: How old is that?

PHYLLIS: Fifty-two.

SALLY: Not old at all. A good time as any to start.

PHYLLIS: But I never went anywhere alone at all. Before I was married, I always traveled with my parents, and after I was married then my husband and I were always together on trips. After my husband died, I traveled with my children. But now they are all grown and have their own families.

SALLY: Maybe you should get a friend to go with you?

PHYLLIS: There's really no one I know who is free to travel. Most of my friends are married and go with their husbands.

SALLY: Who made the rule that you can't strike out alone?

PHYLLIS: Oh, I just can't.

SALLY: Why not?

PHYLLIS: I'd feel like a tramp.

SALLY: What's a tramp?

PHYLLIS: Well, a tramp is a woman who is obviously alone—strolling places alone, eating alone, going into a bar alone—all these things. A woman without a man.

SALLY: So, if two women are together, they're two tramps hanging out?

PHYLLIS: No—you're only a tramp if you're alone.

SALLY: Where is that carved in marble?

PHYLLIS: Well, I just think so. It's how I was brought up. Nice women don't go places alone.

SALLY: You know, we all have to get older physically, but there's none of us has to age mentally. You better make sure that your thoughts are up-to-date, or you're going to miss out on a lot. If you take the attitude that there's something wrong with being alone, think of how lovely and vulnerable some people can look when alone. Most human beings are kind to other human beings, and are friendly and helpful. If you are afraid of looking alone, consider that someone might be very attracted to just that fact. Besides, it's only you who are labeling yourself a tramp, and even if others do see you as being alone, why do you need the approval of all the people you might meet on a weekend that you choose to spend alone? Are you ever going to see them again? Are they ever going to have a part in your life? Who are you worried about? You're worried about going away for a weekend to a strange place—do you think that everybody there is going to somehow impress your life? No way.

PHYLLIS: You're right, Sally. I hadn't thought of it that way.

SALLY: The lovely thing about going off for a weekend alone is that you can play any role you want to play. You can be anybody you want to be and you don't have to impress anyone. You can be yourself and hang what anyone thinks. These people you are going to come in contact with are only so many bit actors in *your* play.

PHYLLIS: Do you really think I can do it?

SALLY: Yes, indeed. Reorganize your thinking about what it means to be a woman alone. Forget that idea that it is somehow naughty. Men don't have that problem—because they are used to being on the prowl. They go off for a weekend alone and they're *looking*. Or they go to the corner bar for a beer, and they don't think anyone is staring at them and wondering why they're alone. It's all in your mind. And you have control of that.

PHYLLIS: I'm going to do it, Sally! Thanks a lot.

If you're using public transportation, plan your traveling to coincide with rush hour. The crowded Friday night ski train is a great place to start meeting people for the weekend, but by Saturday morning, it's all over. Return late. Don't worry so much about Monday morning's alarm clock. You can always catch up on your sleep. The old question ploy is the best way to start a conversation with anyone. Ask any question about the event or activity going on, and make sure you have at least half a dozen follow-up questions to keep the ball rolling.

For example, instead of saying "Where can I get bus number thirty-two?" ask "Are you taking bus thirty-two?" *Then* you can ask where it leaves from, or say something like, "May I walk along with you since you know the way?" Do make sure that your comments are appropriate to the situation.

Feel free to ask to be included in a group doing something or going somewhere. Most people are sociable, and if you don't ask they may assume you want to be alone. When I was on a publicity tour in Florida I discovered that a group from the meeting I had addressed that afternoon was going to a concert. I asked them if I could go along. They said yes, and a ticket was found for me at the hotel's service desk. It hadn't occurred to them to invite me simply because they had just assumed I was tired and might want to be alone. I didn't and I said so. Too often we feel and let ourselves be left out because we don't speak up and let others know we are there and would like to be included.

Memorize these points:

1. Do your homework. Find out what's going on around you.
2. Be as active in seeking out new experiences and places as you can.
3. Plan your weekend time in advance.

4. Budget if you need to—spend money on gas to get there and take an inexpensive room. You don't have to eat in restaurants. Pack a lunch, or buy bread, fruit and cheese along the way.
5. *Talk to strangers*. I can't emphasize this one enough.
6. Stay within your "comfort range" physically, but don't be afraid to be adventurous.

That's it for love on weekends! Now, what about vacations?

21

Looking on Vacations

ONE NIGHT LATE in August a woman named Marilee called me—in tears.

Marilee had scrimped and saved all year for her fabulous vacation. Even though her previous vacations had proved somewhat disappointing (she'd met men, but it hadn't worked out), she had not given up. All year long she had thought about finding love during her next vacation.

When she called me she was overwhelmed by the experience she'd had. A travel agent had talked her into buying a very expensive cruise, and she had been beguiled by the pictures of elegantly dressed men smiling down at beautifully gowned women on a white boat sparkling with lights. She had imagined herself one of its romantic passengers, as it steamed through starlit nights in tropical waters. She bought the fantasy. Literally. She booked a Class A stateroom and went out and purchased a whole new wardrobe— from poolside wear to long evening dresses.

But what Marilee *didn't* do (and hadn't done in previous years!) was her homework. And she found herself at sea in more ways than one. Of her fellow mates, 85 percent were women, all looking for love!

SALLY'S BASIC RULE

Do your homework. Don't leave town until you are fully informed about the situation you're going to face. Work with your travel agent. Ask questions. Talk to others who've been there. Find out what your options are if you book a tour that doesn't turn out the way you expected it to. As the Boy Scouts say, "Be Prepared!"

If, instead of imagining herself standing on the ship's deck in a flowing evening gown with her arms around her future husband, Marilee had checked out the facts of the cruise, she might have saved not only her tears but her precious time and money.

By the way, now is the place for me to tell you that I have *never* met or talked to *anyone* who found love on a cruise ship. Cruises are relaxing and peaceful, the food is often superb, there's lots to do on board and lots to see on land trips, *but* they are not good places to spend your vacation money to find love.

I *do* recommend tours, however, for people traveling to a country they have never visited before. I took a tour on my first trip to Europe. However, you must ask the travel agent frankly about the tour and find out what the prospects are for single people. The travel agent should know if the tour is going to be couples, octogenarians, and so forth. If he or she can't tell you about the company you'll be keeping, don't book the tour. It might turn out to be a disaster and a waste of precious money. *Make sure you know before you go.*

Tours today are highly specialized and are known to attract certain types of people. The more you know about what you want and who you'd like to meet, the better equipped you will be to choose a tour. Don't take the random shot. Again, *do your homework*. There are wine tours, history tours, art tours, cooking lesson tours, music festival tours—and so on. A vacation can be just a nice rest and some new sights, or it can be a richly rewarding experience. It's up to you. The more you know, the better off you are.

I don't think that the small, complete package tour is a good place for meeting people. It's too confining. If the average group of twenty is together, everyone does everything together and there's no chance to go off and meet others. The kind of tour that I prefer is one that gives the tourist the advantage economically of the low-cost airfare of the group, the hotels, and the transfers to and from the airports. Everything else the traveler designs for him/herself. This kind of tour gives the most latitude and flexibility. If you meet someone you'd like to spend time with, you're not bound by an already paid dinner at the hotel or some restaurant. The only thing you need to do is to catch up to the ongoing travel arrangements. You're free to accompany the group on excursions or to go exploring on your own.

As much as your finances will allow, try to take the top-of-the-line tour. The larger companies—American Express, Pan America, and the like—are more likely to give good service than the fly-by-night chartered tour with separate land arrangements. And generally the more expensive your tour is, the more chances you are going to have for finding love.

Choose the most exotic, out-of-the-way places—don't beat the well-worn paths. Unless you are a very conventional person, don't make that umpteenth trip to Italy just because you know a nice little pension there. Avoid the worst tourist traps, the so-called "musts." Unless you have seen nothing at all of Europe (in which case do a quickie tour to discover which parts appeal to you especially), avoid the major capitals in the high season. Paris in August, for example, is deserted except for the tourists, mostly Japanese these days. Italy in August is a madhouse—they call it *ferroagusto,* which simply means that the whole nation is on vacation in its own country, for Italians as a rule don't travel to foreign countries. On the other hand, you'll find six million Dutch in Spain in August during the school vacation time.

I'm often asked about places off the beaten path that are good bets for finding love. There are many of them, and more investigating needs to be done, but here's a short list of those I personally can recommend to anyone seriously looking for love on vacations.

Ireland is a great place. The men are charming (and plentiful). The women are lovely. The great thing about the Irish male is adaptability. He's at home anywhere instantly—very transplantable.

Finland and Norway are great places for ladies looking for men. For some reason, there's a real woman shortage in these cold northern countries, and the men are stalwart and serious.

Scotland is another great place to meet people of either sex.

In *England,* go to the Midlands. Cambridge is nice also—to meet men (and they are all going to speak English!). See especially the lovely Lake District. On Lake Windemere, for example, on a one hour boat ride you're sure to meet someone. And don't forget London—a great place for meeting both sexes!

France is a great place for the young to seek out companionship, especially Mont St. Michel. Older people are better off sticking to where the business people congregate, such as Dijon and Lyon.

Italy's Lake Como is a delight for anyone under twenty-five. If you are older, try Bologna, the high point of Italian cuisine.

Germany is friendliest in the south, though small towns are usually welcoming and you can always strike up an acquaintance on a train. Munich, with its university and concentration on the arts is a good bet. A stroll through the English Gardens of a fine afternoon will put you in touch with many people.

Austria offers romantic Vienna, where it is said even a woman of seventy is expected to have a lover! And Innsbruck is a wonderful place for the young to meet—very open and friendly. Also Salzburg.

Switzerland, the German part especially, is ideal. Train service is super, towns are small, and the people are friendly.

Egypt is a marvellous place for an American woman who wants to get married. One of its great advantages is that Egyptians like their women a good twenty pounds heavier than is the vogue in the U.S.A.! And nearly everybody speaks English.

Greece is a wonderful place for ladies looking for men on the macho side, but beware the gigolo types.

Caribbean Islands to be aware of are:

British West Indies
   Virgin Gorda
   Peter Island (especially the man-filled yacht club)
   Tortula

Grenadines
   St. Vincent's
   Bequia

A good travel agent can give you specific information about what to expect from the different locales, but again your own research is probably the most reliable. Get out there and *ask*. Visit tourist information centers and consulates.

SALLY'S PRIVATE TIP

If you're looking for a king or a millionaire, or a movie queen or a star, there's one place I can recommend you go above all others. It's Gstaad, Switzerland.

This little tiny town has only one street, but it's filled to the brim with wealthy tourists and residents. Famous movie stars and the super rich have villas there.

The best time to go is December, January or February. The place is so small that no one is a stranger. In restaurants you talk from table to table—in fact, you practically pass the mustard from table to table. It's that cozy.

The stores where people pick up their sporting clothes are small and compact, an excellent place to start a conversation. People stroll in the middle of the streets chatting, as hotels are few and guesthouses are many. Everyone's treated as an equal, so you're sure to be included in the activities of the rich and famous. All you have to be is attractive and agreeable!

Americans considering foreign vacations often ask me about the language barrier.

Take Marilyn, for example.

SALLY: Hi! What can I do for you?

MARILYN: Hi, Sally. I'm about to go off on my first trip to Europe and I wondered if you could give me some tips. I'm hoping to meet some interesting people—maybe even find a boyfriend—but I don't speak any languages. I wondered if you could tell me how to turn my lack of languages into an advantage, as I'll be looking for romance, too.

SALLY: You can't do it. I'm sorry to say, but that's a danger. Anyone struggling with a strange language looks cute and charming. But there's positively no way you can judge sincerity, or intelligence, or sensitivity. If you don't have a language in common, and by the way, many, many Europeans do speak English, you're courting trouble.

MARILYN: Then what do I do if I'm attracted to someone who doesn't speak good English?

SALLY: The only thing I can tell you in that case is that you must double, even triple, the time you spend with them before you make any judgment. Because if you can only really understand one hour out of a three-hour date, it's going to take a lot longer to get things clear.

MARILYN: Okay, thanks. That's really good to know about.

Resorts are another popular vacation alternative. Do be certain that you don't pick *either* a family or a singles resort. Again, do your homework. I've been told that dude ranches are good places—but, frankly, I find them tacky. If anyone out there knows anything to the contrary, please pick up your pen or phone and tell me so.

Places where there are horses are good bets, as well as:

- Camera safaris
- Bird watching camps
- Fitness vacations
- Wilderness experiences (Outward Bound, etc.)
- Windjammer-sail and bike-tour combination

- Learning-to-sail vacations
- Physical exercise vacations, such as mountain climbing
- Tennis vacations
- Water-sports lesson/vacations
- Foreign language vacations
- Domestic cruises on rivers and lakes
- Music festivals
- Opera festivals
- Garden tours
- Historical tours
- Old homes tours
- Biking cross-country trips
- Cooking lesson vacations
- Any special interest group.

Whatever your interest, there's bound to be some group or tour connected with it. *If you don't now do so, subscribe to any publications connected with your special interest or hobby.*

Your company or corporation may also sponsor vacations, as may a university nearby. There are all sorts of university-sponsored trips that can put you in contact with like-minded individuals, such as archeological trips where the tourist goes as part of a working archeological team and gets in on the dig as well as experiencing the different surroundings.

Let me tell you about Dan and Carol. He was an engineer with a strong interest in American Indian artifacts. She was a teacher. Both chose an archeological tour sponsored by a Southwestern university that went to sites in Arizona and New Mexico on authentic digs. They met while washing the newly dug treasures, and as the days wore on under the hot sun, their romance blossomed.

There are various types of semi-working vacations for the kind of person who likes a more stimulating time than flaking out on the beach for two weeks, and I highly recommend them as a way for you to meet people of similar interests, education and background.

Wherever you go (unless, as mentioned in the case of packages), pick the larger accommodations. If, say, you have a choice of hotels in the Catskills or the Poconos, take the biggest one. Why? It's simple: there are more people, and that's what looking for love on vacation is all about—meeting as many people as you can in the hope of finding that special one.

Whatever you do, you're playing a numbers game. Go where you are most likely to find more members of the opposite sex. It's entirely fair and reasonable to ask your travel agent frank questions about the availability of men/women at any place you contemplate going. Don't be shy. Knowledge is power, and the more information you accumulate before you step on that plane, train, bus, or auto, the better your chances of finding love.

I'm often asked what clothing to take on vacation. Naturally, this depends a great deal upon the climate, time of year, et cetera—but one piece of advice I can give is to take *fun* clothes (that wildly printed shirt that you secretly love but everyone makes fun of, for example). Vacations are a time to loosen up, right? Nobody knows you, you don't have a reputation preceding you . . . live it up a little!

But again, I do suggest that *comfort* be your priority in choosing your traveling wardrobe. Don't get caught up worrying about fashion and fad. If you're going to be in cities, dress accordingly, but keep it simple. The layering principle works for just about every climate, season and locale, for males and females alike. If it's cooler, you add another layer; warmer, take one off. Stick to one or two basic colors with no more than two accessory colors and you'll find your wardrobe coordinated. Don't take a bunch of different outfits that need special accessories. Be sensible. Include rainwear (even if you don't want to *consider* the possibility that it might rain) and any special cosmetics or medicines you won't be able to obtain elsewhere. If you wear glasses, take an extra pair—especially if you need them for driving. Make sure you have comfortable walking shoes—pinched and hurting feet have ruined the best-planned vacation of many a weary traveler.

As for Club Med locations, the farther afield you go, the more exotic the place, the most serious are the people looking for mates. Those at Maui and Marrakech are better than the ones in the U.S., Mexico, and the Caribbean. The latter draw a very young crowd, more interested in one-night stands than seriously looking for love.

The Club Med copy, Hedonist, is also not recommended. They are very young, favoring casual sex. There's a party atmosphere to these places, a kind of once-a-year-day cutting loose before it's back-to-Boston-and-button-up. Thus, the real person isn't on display, but a vacationized version which, like those shells on the beach that are so pretty when they're wet and shining, but look dull and uninteresting back home.

Another disadvantage to these types of clubs is the isolation. If you're not happy and don't find anyone to suit you, you are stuck. There's just no place else to go, and you've already paid your money. So take care in your choice. Your travel agent and the club itself have statistics on age, marital status, occupations of the people who frequent each location. Demand precise information.

Let me tell you about the way *I* travel. People in the broadcasting business are often invited on tours by governments who hope we will promote tourism to their countries.

So whatever industry you are in, investigate the tours available to you. The same goes for any societies or groups you have joined. The Japan club I belong to is always offering special offers for touring Japan at bargain rates, for example. The best place for you to shine is in your own field of endeavor. Look to industry newsletters and trade papers for information about such tours and vacations, and take advantage of them.

My last tip to the seriously-looking-for-love person is to

take frequent vacations. The more often the better. If you have a month off, don't use it all up on some grand tour. Budget half of that time for extra-long weekends, or break it up into four separate weeks. Take time in winter and summer if you possibly can. Spread it out for the best mileage. Keep moving. Cover as much territory as you can.

With your awareness high and your eyes open, your designs clear and your priorities set, you'll be putting yourself into a wonderful mood to go looking for love on vacation time. Happy hunting!

22

Looking Again

SO YOU FOUND love and now it's gone. You've been dumped. Or you're divorced. Maybe widowed. You're burned, depressed, certainly lonely. Worse, you may be over thirty. And you may have children to cope with. What now?

First, get rid of that person who has left you or whom you've left. I know you're alone—but if that other person is still there in your mind or in your life, you're not ready to begin again. I call this a "love hangover."

You have a love hangover if:

- You hang on to old friends you don't really care for hoping to find out what he/she is doing.
- You hang out at the old haunts that used to be your favorites with him/her.
- You hang on to old patterns—any ex who goes on fixing the car, minding the bookkeeping, or otherwise performing chores for the other isn't out of the relationship, even if he/she has final divorce papers.
- You are still living in the same house "for financial reasons."

- You feel that your ex still needs you—whether for some task like house repairs or clothes shopping.
- You feel that you "owe" your ex something because he/she is helpless without you.

Beware of these behavior patterns in a prospective partner as well. They mean trouble. Even the most clear-headed among us have emotional rubbish inside, holding on to an old or fairy-tale image of love and romance. Sometimes they find a new partner, and then when some over-idealized image doesn't come along with the relationship, they go sour and find reasons to terminate it, landing just where they were before. Often a love hangover is the culprit.

Naturally, a person who has been married may still be feeling the bruises, and depending on how long he/she has been divorced or separated, this is normal. But if an "ex" is always creeping into your conversation or calling up on the phone, or you're a frequent caller, take immediate action.

If there are children involved, plan to make them a part of a relationship, when you can without interfering with the level of intimacy. However, if your children object to a new partner, remember that your primary responsibility is to your own life. One day they will be gone and living their own lives.

One of the biggest problems I encounter in answering America's questions about love is what I have come to call "romantic thinking." This is the idea—and believe me it affects men as well as women (though women are its worst victims)—that there is *one* partner or mate out there in all this whole wide world for you alone. 'T'ain't so.

Promise yourself a fresh start. And mean it. You deserve it. No matter how awful you're feeling now, it's *never* too late to find love. You're entitled to your mistakes. Usually the first big one comes early. If this is *your* first, chalk it up to experience, and learn from it.

The romantic fallacy, which we are fed daily in large doses by the media—TV, movies, romance novels, happy marriage celebrity stories—and even seems to be in the air we breathe, does a lot of damage to our emotional lives, as does clinging to the past.

Take Louisa. When she called me for advice she said she was looking for new love, but couldn't find it. She had traveled, had various jobs, and circulated socially. Still, nothing. I asked how long she had been divorced. Ten years. Was her husband remarried? No, he wasn't. In fact, they still dated occasionally and he had offered her a job in his new business. She was thrilled.

Something was clearly wrong with this equation—but what?

Some gentle probing uncovered a surprising fact: though Louisa and her husband had been *separated* for ten years and divorce papers had been filed for seven of them, neither party had ever finalized the divorce! In addition, they still shared property.

Though Louisa chose to see the situation as merely one of convenience, saying that neither she nor her husband had "bothered" to pick up the divorce papers from the lawyer and sign them (though they had been ready and waiting for seven years), it was clear to me that they were both holding on to an old situation. Unable to live together, wanting other partners, they had nonetheless chosen to remain together in a state of marital limbo, attached but unattached. It was no wonder that Louisa couldn't find another man and certainly no surprise that her husband's love affairs fizzled one after the other. Neither one was truly available to another person.

"Well, if I find someone I want to marry, I can always pick up the divorce papers then," said Louisa.

But she will *never* find someone else until she has severed her ties to her ex-husband. Nor will he.

What makes people behave like this? Though admittedly

Louisa's is an extreme case of hanging on to the past,
many of us do it in other, less obvious, ways. An emotional attachment that has meant a great deal is not easy to
cut. But the ties that bind, when they don't bind both
parties anymore, *must* be cut before life can go on.

Even if you have children, the person you had your
children with isn't necessarily the best person for you to
spend the rest of your life with.

Years and years ago, when the life span was a lot
shorter, it made much more sense to pledge "until death
do us part." Today, as we live longer and longer, you may
have to plan for *consecutive* romances over the course of
life. One of the great stumbling blocks that affects the
divorced and widowed, and even the long-term live-ins
who have split, is guilt and self-blame. Especially when
there has been a third party in a divorce or split-up there is
often a great deal of self-castigation on the part of the
person left.

"Why couldn't I have been all he/she needed/wanted?"
is the familiar lament. As if the marriage ceremony had
cast both people in cement! Personally, from long experience I don't think that there is any "one and only" for
anyone. We change too much over the course of a life;
other people change too much. What you were at twenty,
you are not at thirty. Sometimes people grow together at
the same rate, but rarely. When it happens that you or your
partner has outgrown the relationship, the only thing to do
is accept that fact and go on.

SALLY'S BASIC RULE

Don't limit yourself to the idea of one life–one love.
Plan to have at least four important loves in your
life.

Becoming defensive because of being hurt is okay for a little while, but the romantic hangover must be cured for another love to take its place, just as the dead bloom must be removed for another to grow.

Let's face it, if you're alive and kicking out there you are bound to get hurt emotionally at some time in your life. Most love does not end well. I'm sorry if that sounds like a terribly cynical viewpoint, but it happens to be the truth. And maybe if you keep that in mind the next time around it will help you. Sentimental fantasies about "this time it will be perfect" won't help.

Yet, setting up a defense against being hurt—vowing never to love again, planning not to let yourself go completely—doesn't work. Why not? Because you'll never have the joy of loving, and that's one of the biggest highs life has to offer. There's a down side, of course, as there is with anything. But look at it this way. The highs of romance are so wonderful *because* of the lows and the doldrums in between. If you ask me, "Are the highs worth the lows?" I would have to answer *yes* every time. When you're in the low, you don't believe it, but when you're in the high you *know* it's true.

How to get rid of the love hangover? Remember when I talked about grief? Well, that's just what you must do. Grieve. Allow yourself all the time you need. Have a pity party for yourself. Don't stint. You haven't really earned your stripes in life until you've gone round the block three or four times.

Let me turn to you women for a moment. You've gotten over your love hangover, you take a deep breath, and you're ready to look again . . . until you hear those gloomy statistics on the male/female ratio. Well, I can look those statistics right in their bleary eye and say, "Lady, if you truly want love and you are willing to do what's necessary, you can have it."

And I do *not* mean compromising your integrity or

stooping to male-flattering devices of deception, as advised by some current gurus of romance. I hereby reject categorically the notion that a woman (of any age) is better off with a man (of any sort or calibre) than alone. If you are going to be alone, you can still live a high quality life, with your freedom and integrity intact. The idea that *anybody* is better than *nobody* is simply not correct. *Nobody* is better than just *anybody*.

Yes, older women do have a harder time finding love, and I won't deny that. But, like anything else, the more you have to work for something, the more you value it. And the more careful you are with how you use it.

Men can learn to treasure the love of a mature woman. We talk blithely about the divorce rate and the emotional damage as if it affects only women. Men are one half of the statistics and they get very little sympathy for their condition. An older woman is in the perfect position to be a lover, companion, and *teacher*.

Although I can't change the statistics for women, I can hope to help them change their *attitude* about how they go looking for new love. What this means is that every woman who genuinely wants to find love needs to put effort into the job. We've talked about getting ready, and making love your first priority. Women who are looking the second, third, or fourth time around need to learn to be more assertive than they are accustomed to being. The most important thing I'm going to tell women who are looking again is that it's perfectly proper—even necessary—for the gal to do the courting. The days when a woman could sit with her hands folded in her lap and wait for a "gentleman caller" have gone the way of the horse and buggy.

Let me give you an example.

Jessica was forty-two. She'd been widowed and had no children, but she felt that her age put her out of the running and she had resigned herself to living alone. A piano teacher, she loved music and went weekly to the Boston Symphony when it was in season.

One evening, as the orchestra was tuning up, her friend Elaine, who shared a subscription with her, asked, "Jessica, what would you like for your birthday?"

Offhandedly, Jessica answered, "Him," pointing to the second cellist, a robust, bearded, teddy-bear-of-a-man in his mid-thirties.

On Jessica's birthday, a few days later, Elaine invited her for lunch, and handed her a slip of paper.

"Here's his name, address, and phone number," she said triumphantly.

"Whose?" Jessica asked, puzzled.

"The cellist you wanted for your birtliday."

Flustered, Jessica waved the paper.

"How'd you get it?" she asked suspiciously.

Elaine laughed.

"You forget I'm on the board of the symphony!"

"Oh, of course. But, Elaine, what am I suppose to do?

"Call him."

"I can't do that! He'd think I was crazy."

"Then write him a note. Invite him to tea. I got the information. The rest is up to you."

"I can't just pop up out of the blue and invite him—it wouldn't be proper."

"Nonsense. You can do as you like. You're a grown woman."

The end of the story is that Jessica did what Elaine advised. She telephoned him and told him how much she enjoyed his playing, inviting him for afternoon tea. At this writing, they have been happily married for eight years!

What if she had let that opportunity pass by because she thought it "wasn't proper" to court a man?

But many women who are looking for love the second time around remain mired in the old ideas.

Here are some that need to be scratched—*fast*.

1. A man should be at least a few inches taller and *a few years older* than a woman. *False*.
2. It's improper and unfeminine for a woman to show interest in a man before he shows interest in her. *False*.
3. It's not nice for a woman to telephone a man and ask for a date. *False*.
4. Women have to pretend to be other than they are; that is, weaker, less smart, nonassertive, in order for men to like them. *False*.
5. Men aren't interested in women with children. *False*. There are just as many men who like children and want the whole package as there are who refuse the responsibility.

You can make your own list. A little self-examination will tell you just what you need to change.

Get rid of your old, outworn notions about a man being the end-all and the be-all of life. Get your own life full and crackin'. The more you have going for you in your own life, the less you will *need* a man. And the less you need, the easier it will be to get what you *want*.

My strongest advice to you is: *learn to talk to strangers*. I've said it before, and I'll continue to say it until you hear me out there in Americaland. On buses, on trains, in lines at the supermarket, at shopping malls, in the park, at museums, at the zoo—anywhere and everywhere you go. *Talk to strangers*.

You men need reprogramming, too. So many of you call me to ask where to find a woman . . . well, I say—widen your horizons. Get rid of those old notions of what a woman is all about. Think of her as an equal, not someone to cook your dinner and wash your laundry. The old shibboleths about women just won't do anymore. There's a new crop of young men coming into manhood, and they are going to move right in and challenge their elders. As women become more choosy, they will have more choice.

For both sexes, flexibility is the key. Knowing who you are and what you want, being able to adjust to what is available, being willing to go afield to find what you need, shaking off those old ideas of male/female roles and updating attitudes and expectations.

The older you get, the more experience you have, and the more opportunity you have to choose instead of being chosen, to be in charge of your life instead of letting the winds of chance rule you.

Once you've decided that you want love again, you can have it—if you're willing to do the work.

And remember what's been said about love being even *better* the second time around!

It's never too late to find love! Single people of all ages—over forty, over fifty, over sixty, over seventy—are dating and looking for love. They're finding it, too, and so can you! And falling in love at any age is just as exciting as it was when you were young. As one man said, "Love is when you look at the other person and your heart just beats faster." He was sixty-five. What do older couples do on dates? Everything that younger ones do.

One woman, Eileen, fifty-six, met a man while she was on vacation with her school-age son. A widow, she'd been busy rearing her youngest boy and reactivating a career. Then, on a ferryboat in Scotland, there was Roger. He, too, was vacationing with his youngest son. They struck up a friendship that continued and soon a business trip brought him to the United States to visit her from his home in England. Next, they arranged to share a ski vacation apartment during the boys' school vacation. After that, he invited her on a vacation trip to Hawaii, where whey discussed the possibility of setting up housekeeping together. Next, she decided to go spend a month in England as a trial period to see how they would work out living together. It's been fun all the way.

Older people enjoy the romantic trappings of dating just as much as younger ones do—and they are just as interested in sex, too.

There's a saying that "hope springs eternal in the human breast," and this applies to love. People, no matter how old they are, are always looking for love. And finding it, too!

On Your Own:
Your Personal Game Plan

I want to tell you about Wayne, a shy dairy farmer in Wisconsin.

Wayne called me a couple of years ago. He told me that he was unmarried, in his thirties, and wanted to find love. Trouble was, he hadn't the faintest idea how to go about it.

So I started him on my plan. Over a period of two years, I led Wayne by the hand, so to speak, over the radio, introducing him to my personal plan for finding love.

We went step-by-step. We discussed attitude, fitness, health, wardrobe. I got him On the Mark. We went through the process of Getting Set, Getting Ready, to Go.

Wayne would call and ask my advice every week or so and I taught him to analyze his style, his character, think about age. We talked about how he spent his money and how to increase his opportunities by becoming interested in other things beyond cows and feed.

As time passed, I came to look forward to Wayne's calls—and to learn about his progress. There were a couple of false starts, after which I talked to him about his fantasy and how to cope with rejection. Though he had never been married, there was an old thorn in his heart, and I told him how to take it out.

First dates were always a problem for Wayne—he felt tense and awkward, and I helped him to realize that a first date is just that—a first date. A trial run. And trial runs are just to size up the situation.

Finally, Wayne called and told me that he felt he was really ready—but there just didn't seem to be anyone around who was both available and suitable.

Well, I taught him how to look at home and then he broadened out to looking on weekends. He didn't take many business trips, but there was the occasional State Fair or local convention, and I got him to think about how these could expand his opportunities.

Mostly I kept his spirits up as he found his way along the not-always-easy path to finding love. He took frequent vacations, and his experiences made him more self-confident and made talking to strangers much easier for him.

Well, I have to tell you it was a thrill for me when Wayne called recently *to invite me to his wedding!* Yes, you heard right. Wayne found love by following the very plan you've been reading. And I'll be flying out to Wisconsin to witness his success.

I'm Sally Jessy Raphael . . . and that's a wrap!
Keep those success stories coming in.

SALLY JESSY RAPHAEL, a veteran broadcaster, is the host of her own syndicated TV talk show, *The Sally Jessy Raphael Show,* which originates in New Haven, Connecticut and is heard nationwide. She is also host of a popular nightly call-in talk show on ABC radio network, which airs from New York City. Monday through Friday, for three hours live each evening, Sally gives advice to her callers from all over the country about love and relationships, jobs and careers, and other topics of concern to her listeners. Previously, she was host of *Talknet* on NBC radio network.

M. J. ABADIE is a holistic psychotherapist and professional astrological counsellor with a private practice in Manhattan. She specializes in relationships, personal growth, and creative development. In addition to her work as a writer of fiction and non-fiction, she is a designer, painter, and mask-maker with a keen interest in all the arts.